Hey there, future paper airplane pilot! Are you ready Paper Airplane Origami? Imagine being able to fold into an awesome flying machine that soars through magic, but it's real!

Origami is a super cool art form all about folding paper to create amazing things. And when it comes to paper airplanes, it's even more fun! With just a few folds and a little bit of imagination, you can make all sorts of different planes that zoom, glide, and loop through the sky.

So, grab some paper and get ready to embark on an exciting adventure in Paper Airplane Origami! Let's fold, fly, and see where our imaginations take us! Are you ready for takeoff? Let's go!

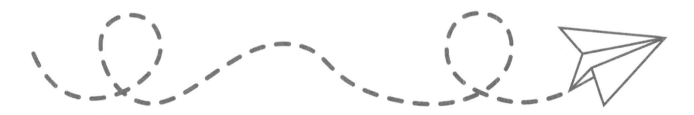

HOW TO USE THE ARROWS

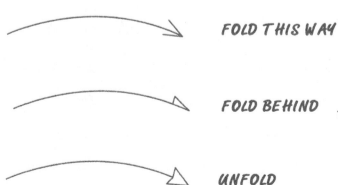

FOLD THIS WAY

FOLD BEHIND

UNFOLD

Fold lines are like the secret codes of origami! They're super important because they tell us exactly where to fold our paper to make amazing creations. Paying close attention to these fold lines will help you understand how to make basic origami shapes. With a little focus and some careful folding, you'll soon become a master of paper airplanes!

How do Airplanes Stay in the Air?

The key is finding the right balance among four essential forces: thrust, drag, lift, and gravity.

Thrust is the force that propels the plane forward. In the world of paper airplanes, it's the energy from your arm when you launch the plane. Drag, on the other hand, is what slows the plane down, caused by the air's friction against it. Lift is the upward force that prevents the plane from falling, while gravity pulls it downward. The secret to keeping an airplane airborne is maintaining harmony among these factors. Remarkably, these principles apply equally to massive jetliners and simple paper airplanes.

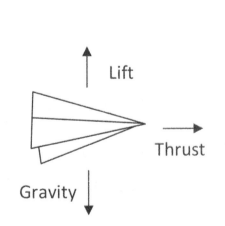

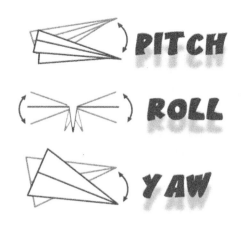

PITCH

ROLL

YAW

In the realm of paper airplanes, stability is crucial for smooth flight—meaning the plane travels in a straight line without tilting, diving, or veering. Rotations, such as pitch (nose angle), roll (wing levelness), and yaw (side-to-side motion), influence stability. Pitch relates to the nose pointing up or down, roll to the wings' levelness, and yaw to side-to-side motion.

The flight of your paper plane depends on its design and launch. Even after completion, you can alter its flight path by tweaking its structure or adjusting your throwing technique. If your plane spins or turns unexpectedly, check the symmetry of the wings' levelness. A nosedive can be countered by curling the wingtips for added lift. Start with subtle adjustments and experiment with gentle and strong throws, different angles, and wing configurations. The key is to observe how each change affects the flight.

Let's Make The *Aero Arrow*

Difficulty

★★★★★ 1.5

Why did the paper airplane go to school?
Because it wanted to be a high-flyer!
What do you call a paper airplane that can't fly?
Stationery!
I'm made of paper, light as can be,
Fold me just right, and watch me flee.
I soar through the air, with grace and style,
But I'm just a sheet, not a mile.
What am I?

Step 1:
Take your sheet of paper and fold it in half from left to right, making sure both sides are even. Then, unfold it when you're done.

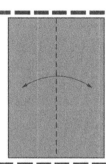

Step 2:
Next, bring the top right edge of the paper to the left side and match them together, just like in the picture.

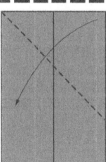

Step 3:
Now, it's time to fold the top left edge to the right side triangle end.

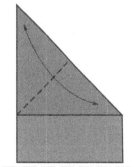

Step 4:
Fold down the nose of the paper airplane to the bottom of the triangle along the dotted line in the center like this.

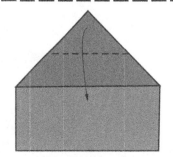

Aero Arrow

Step 5:
Fold the paper airplane in half from left to right, making sure both sides match up perfectly.

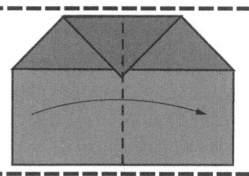

Step 6:
Fold the wings down on both sides, about 1 inch from the bottom. You can refer to the picture if you need help.

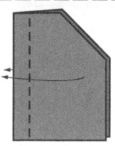

Step 7:
Winglets are important for stabilizing your aircraft. Fold the edges of the wings on both sides upward, about half an inch, to make winglets. You can compare step 7 and step 8 for guidance.

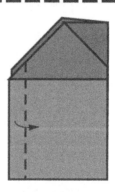

Step 8:
This paper airplane loves its wings and performs well in strong winds sometimes!

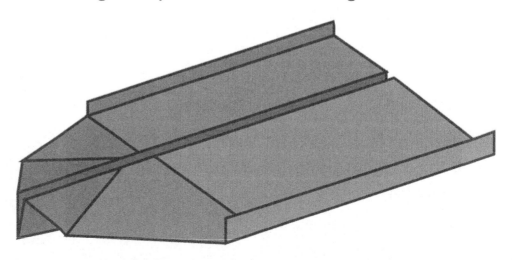

Let's Make The *Aero Glide*

Difficulty

★★★★★ 3.5

The big question is how to make a paper airplane that flies super far and looks awesome – that's what matters to a real airplane expert! What makes you a paper airplane expert? Well, it's all about practicing a lot with origami paper planes and knowing a little bit about the science behind them. There are tons of cool designs out there, like gliders, darts, boomerang airplanes, and more!

Step 1:
Take your sheet of paper and fold it in half from left to right, making sure both sides are even. Then, unfold it when you're done.

Step 2:
Now, bring the top left and top right edges to the center crease, but be careful not to cross the center line.

Step 3:
Bring the top of the paper down to the bottom along the center line, making sure to align the nose with the center. Fold it neatly from the white dot to dot.

Step 4:
Push the nose up to create a full triangle shape, aligning it with the center line as shown here.

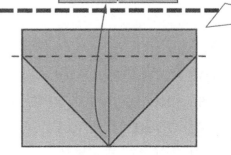

Aero Glide

Step 5:
Fold the right and left side sections along the dotted lines in the center, as shown right here.

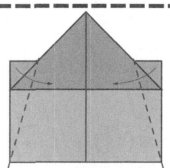

Step 6:
Fold the nose down along the dotted lines in the center.

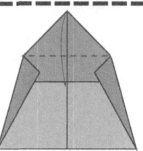

Step 7:
Fold the plane in half along the center line, matching the sides perfectly and carefully to make sure it is even.

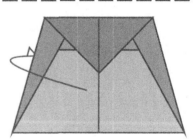

Step 8:
Now, create the wings by folding about 1 inch from the left on both sides of the plane.

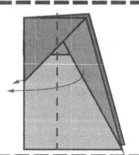

Step 9:
Lift up the wings slightly to make it look like a 'T' from the front view. Your paper airplane is ready to fly far! Find a good spot, like an open ground or school auditorium, and let it soar!

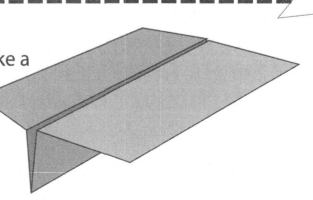

Let's Make The Air Cutter

As a kid, my friends and I were obsessed with making paper airplanes. One day, we had a contest in the park. I confidently launched my plane, only to watch it crash spectacularly. Despite the laughter, I vowed to build an even better one next time. And so, the contest continued, filled with laughter and memories.

Difficulty

★★★★★★ 3.0

Step 1:

Take your sheet and fold it to make a square paper. Then, fold the square paper in half vertically and horizontally, and then unfold it.

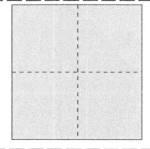

Step 2:

Fold the top edge of the paper down to the center crease, just like the picture shown from dot to dot.

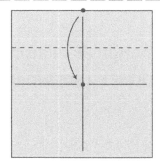

Step 3:

Fold the top right and left corners of the paper down to the center crease.

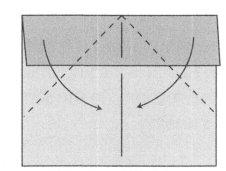

Step 4:

Fold one half of the paper over the other half in the opposite direction. This is called a mountain fold.

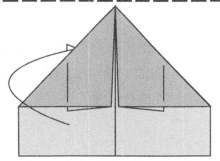

Air Cutter

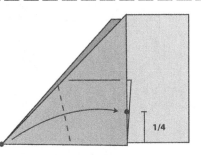

Step 5:
Fold the nose of your cutter plane approximately one-quarter of the way down from the top edge. Look for the dot I've shown you that marks one-quarter of the vertical edge.

Step 6:
Now, unfold it back.

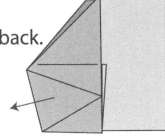

Step 7:
Fold the nose of the plane inside the neck, as shown .

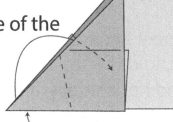

Step 8:
Tuck the extra triangular section inside. Follow the guide lines as you seen shown in the picture.

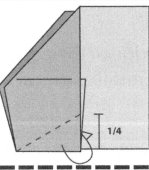

Step 9
Fold down the wings along the dotted line. The dotted lines are a little less than half of the frontal nose section. Do the same for the other side of the wing.

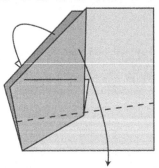

Step 10:
Lift the wings properly, as shown. You've done a wonderful job making this plane! Now, go throw it in the sky!

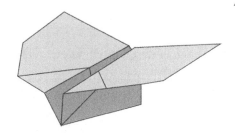

Let's Make The Airborne Ace

I've tried lots of different paper airplane designs, but there's one that I always come back to – the best paper airplane in the world! Even after so many throws, it still flies like a dream. What makes it the best? Well, it's not about flying the farthest or staying in the air the longest. The best paper airplane has to have the perfect balance of both. That way, even a little kid can give it a toss and watch it soar. So let's give it a try and see what we can do!

Difficulty
★ ★ ★ ★ ★ 3.0

Step 1:
Take your sheet of paper and fold it from left to right equally, as shown. Then, unfold it.

Step 2:
Bring the top left and top right edges to the center crease. Make sure not to cross the center line.

Step 3:
Fold the right and left side edges of your triangle to the center line. Make sure the bottom right and left edges are sharp and pointy.

Step 4:
Fold the top-right and top-left edges again to the center line, approximately to the mid-line. You can compare picture 4 and picture 5 for better understanding.

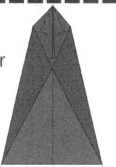

Airborne Ace

Step 5:
Fold the paper airplane in half, creating a mountain fold, as shown.

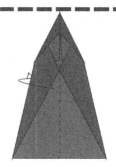

Step 6:
Now, it's time to make the wings. Fold the wings into half on both sides, checking for symmetry if you want it to fly well. But don't worry if you don't plan to fly it – LOL!

Step 7:
Congratulations!
You've successfully made the best paper airplane in the world (for now, at least)! It's great for beginners and performs well with gentle launches. Keep in mind that there's always a new paper plane waiting to take the title, so stay curious! You can also try using dihedral wings for different flight performances.

Let's Make The Boomerang

Boomerang paper airplanes are super fun and easy to make! Unlike regular paper airplanes that fly in a straight line, boomerang paper airplanes have a special trick – they come back to you after every throw! It's like having your own little flying buddy that always comes back for more.

Difficulty

★ ★ ★ ★ ★ 1.5

Cutting a Square:

Keep your sheet vertically like a portrait rectangle over the work table or floor. Grab the top right sharp edge to match the left side of the paper straight. Please refer the picture to the right.

Cut This Off

Step 1:

First, place your square paper flat on the table. Then, fold it from left to right and unfold it back to its original state. This is the first step in making your boomerang airplane.

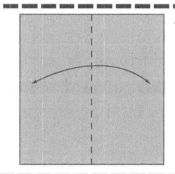

Step 2:

Now, bring the top left and top right corners of the paper to the center line. Make sure they match up perfectly and fold them in.

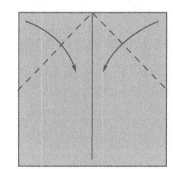

Step 3:

Fold the nose of the paper to meet the center line slightly ahead of the triangle's bottom. If you're unsure, you can compare picture 3 and picture 4 for guidance.

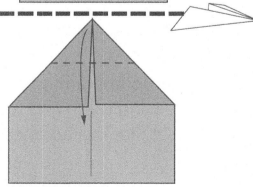

Boomerang

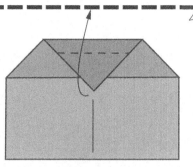

Step 4:
Next, pull up the nose of the paper about one-third of the way up the triangle and fold it over. This is the fourth step in making your boomerang airplane.

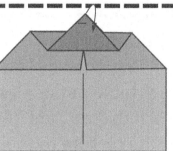

Step 5:
Hold the nose down to a level of about one-fourth of the triangle's height as shown.

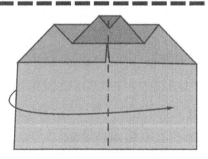

Step 6:
Now, fold the paper airplane in half, with the nose folding inward. Make sure to check for symmetry to ensure your airplane flies well.

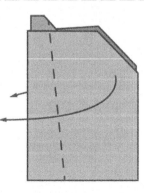

Step 7:
It's time to make the wings! Follow the instructions shown in step 7 and compare them to step 8.

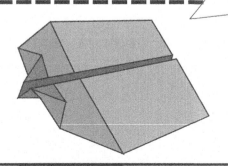

Step 8:
Hold your boomerang airplane at about a 45-degree angle and give it a gentle throw. Watch as it flies in a boomerang motion!

Let's Make The Branson Burner

Ever found yourself in school passing papers to a friend? It's something most of us have tried at least once! But here's a funny twist – why not try passing your message with a paper airplane? Introducing the Branson Burner, your new secret weapon for smoothly gliding information across the room. Curious how it works? Let me show you! With just five easy steps, you'll become a Far Distance Traveller in no time.

Difficulty

★ ★ ★ ★ ★ 0.5

Step 1:

Get a sheet of paper and lay it flat on the table in front of you, with the long side facing you. Fold it in half from right to left so it's like a book.

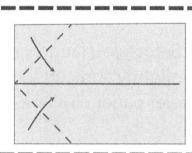

Step 2:

Fold the right and left sides (marked A and B) in towards the center crease, as shown here.

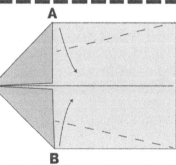

Step 3:

Now, fold the points marked C and D towards the center crease, making sure they don't cross over the line. This will be the body of your traveler plane.

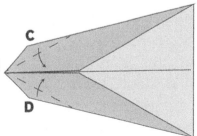

Step 4:

It's time for a mountain fold! Fold your paper along the crease to create a raised shape, getting ready for takeoff.

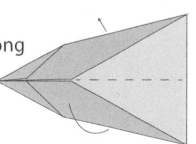

Branson Burner

Step 5:
Fold the wings down to match the bottom center of the fuselage (that's the body of the plane).

Step 6:
Almost there! Before you launch, make sure the wings are angled up slightly and curl the tail points just a little. Now your traveler paper airplane is ready to soar!

Let's Make The BREAKER

Difficulty

★★★★★ 2.5

Long ago, a clever man named Leonardo da Vinci looked up at the birds soaring high in the sky and wondered how they did it. He was so amazed by nature's tricks that he decided to try making his own flying machines. He might have been the very first person to come up with the idea of a glider!

But Leonardo didn't stop there. Oh no! He even tried strapping people onto his gliders and sending them off cliffs to see if they could fly like the birds.

Step 1:
First, place your sheet of paper on the table in portrait orientation. Fold it in half from top to bottom, then unfold it.

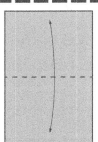

Step 2:
Next, fold the paper from left to right, and then unfold it once you're done.

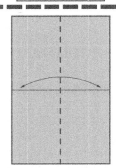

Step 3:
Now, find the center point where the creases meet. Fold the top-right corner to this center point.

Step 4:
Repeat the same step for the top-left corner. Fold it to the center point as well.

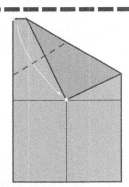

BREAKER

Step 5:
Fold both the right and left edges towards the center line.

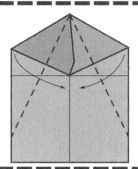

Step 6:
Fold the top edge of the paper down to the backside, leaving about a 1.5-inch gap from the bottom line.

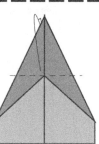

Step 7:
Flip the paper airplane over to the other side.

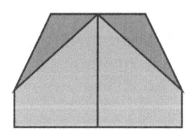

Step 8:
Pull up the nose of the plane, leaving a 1cm gap from the top.

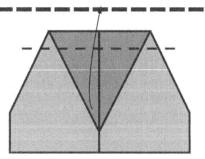

Step 9:
Flip the paper back to the original side.

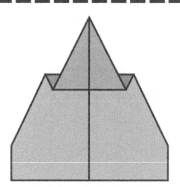

BREAKER

Step 10:
Now, fold the fins on the right and left edges as shown.

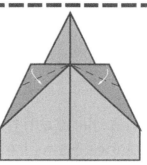

Step 11:
Fold the plane in half along the center crease as the midline.

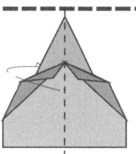

Step 12:
Fold the wings and winglets as shown.

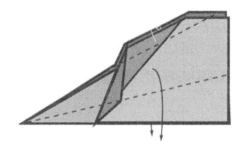

Step 13:
Congratulations! You've successfully created a record-breaking paper airplane model. It performs well and provides a smooth flight experience, especially on gentle launches. Enjoy your flight!

GAMES!

Distance Contest:
See whose paper airplane can fly the farthest. Mark a starting line and take turns launching your planes. Measure the distance each plane travels and declare the winner.

Accuracy Challenge:
Set up a target, such as a hoop or a designated landing area, and take turns trying to land your paper airplanes as close to the target as possible. The player with the most accurate throws wins.

Time Aloft Competition:
Launch your paper airplanes and see whose plane can stay in the air the longest. Time each flight and record the results. The plane that stays aloft for the longest duration wins.

Obstacle Course:
Create an obstacle course using household items like chairs, tables, and books. Take turns navigating your paper airplanes through the course, trying to complete it in the shortest amount of time.

Dogfight Battle:
Equip each player's paper airplane with a paperclip or other lightweight object, then launch them simultaneously. The goal is to knock your opponents' planes out of the air while keeping yours flying. The last plane remaining airborne wins.

Relay Race:
Divide into teams and set up a relay race course. Each team member must launch their paper airplane and then run to a designated point before the next team member can launch their plane. The first team to complete the relay wins.

Let's Make The Breeze Blaster

Are you struggling to make awesome paper airplanes? I used to, too, when I was a kid. But now, with these easy illustrated instructions, I'll never have to struggle again! Making paper airplanes is a fun activity enjoyed by kids all around the world. Did you know that during World War II, the United States made lots of paper toys and airplanes out of available materials?

Difficulty

 ★ ★ ★ ⯪ ★ 3.5

Step 1:
To start, lay your paper flat on a table or surface, making sure it's horizontal. Fold it from left to right, then unfold it back to its original state.

Step 2:
Next, bring the top right and top left corners of the paper to the center crease and fold them in.

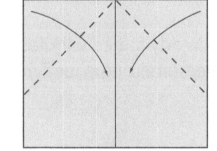

Step 3:
Now, fold the left and right diagonal edges of the paper towards the center crease, creating a point at the top.

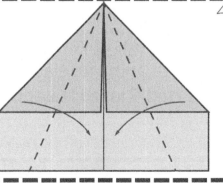

Step 4:
Fold the paper airplane in half along the center crease, following the arrows. Make sure to check that both sides are even.

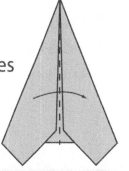

Breeze Blaster

Step 5:
Time to make the wings! Fold down the diagonal sections to create wings about 1 inch from the bottom edge. Repeat this step on both sides.

Step 6:
Now, let's add some winglets for stability. Fold the edges of the wings upwards by about half an inch to create winglets. Look at step 6 and step 7 for help.

Step 7:
Fold the already folded winglets downwards once more, stabilizing your flying paper airplane.

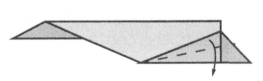

Step 8:
Bring up the wings of your paper airplane to match the size of the fuselage fold. Check step 8 and step 9 for a clearer picture.

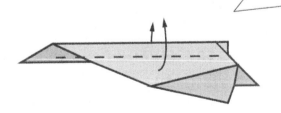

Step 9:
Your Breeze Blaster paper airplane is now ready for action! Find a clear space and let it soar through the sky!

Let's Make The *Breeze Blitzer*

This paper airplane design is super simple with just a few folds, and it flies like a dream right from the start! While there are more advanced designs out there, this one is straightforward and easy to follow. With a perfect toss, it can fly really far and impress all your friends.

Difficulty

★ ★ ★ ★ ★ 2.0

Step 1:
First, place your paper horizontally on a table or flat surface. Fold it from left to right, then unfold it back to its original position.

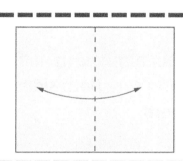

Step 2:
Next, bring the top right and top left corners of the paper to the center crease and fold them in.

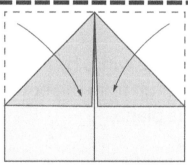

Step 3:
Now, fold the nose of the airplane down to the bottom of the triangle, aligning it with the center line. Make sure to fold it from the dot to dot.

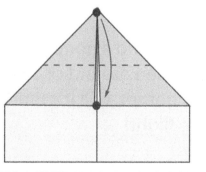

Step 4:
Fold the right and left edges of the paper airplane towards the center line. Be careful not to let them cross the center crease.

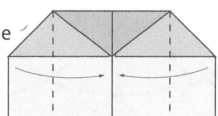

Breeze Blitzer

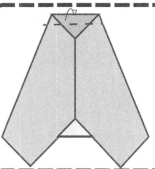

Step 5:
Fold the nose of the airplane back towards the top, covering about half of the top shape. Look at the picture if you need help.

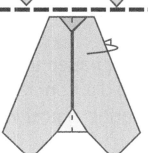

Step 6:
Fold the paper airplane in half along the center crease, making sure both sides are symmetrical (nice and even).

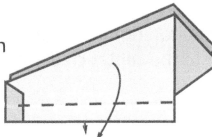

Step 7:
Now, make the wings by folding about an inch of the paper up from the bottom on both sides of the plane.

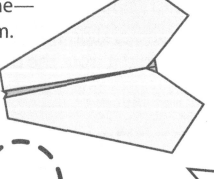

Step 8:
You're all set! Find a good spot to fly your plane—maybe an open ground or a school auditorium. Get ready, get set, GO! It's time to see your plane take flight!

Let's Make The Breeze Brawler

Did you know that launching a paper airplane from high altitudes, like mountains, can make them travel even farther? It's true! They soar through the air for long distances, just like real airplanes.

And here's a fun fact: When the Wright brothers made their first successful flight, they made sure to apply all their knowledge of paper airplane building to make sure everything was perfect. Who knew paper airplanes could teach us so much?

Difficulty

★ ★ ★ ★ ★ 2.0

Step 1:
First, take your sheet of paper and fold it from left to right equally, just like this. Then, unfold it back to its original state.

Step 2:
Now, bring the top left and top right edges of the paper to the center crease. Make sure they meet perfectly without crossing the center line.

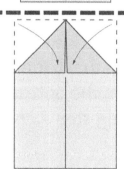

Step 3:
Fold the top-left and top-right diagonal edges of the paper to the center crease, as shown here. Once you're done, unfold them back.

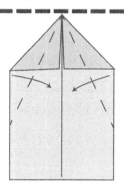

Step 4:
Flip the plane over to the other side.

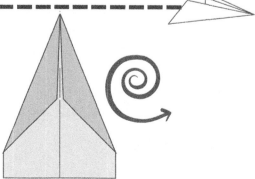

Breeze Brawler

Step 5:
Fold the nose of the plane down so that it covers about 50% of the triangle shape, following the dots here. It should end looking like step 6.

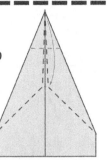

Step 6:
Fold the paper airplane in half along the center crease, creating a mountain fold. Make sure both sides are symmetrical (even).

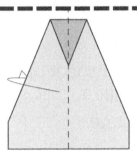

Step 7:
Now, fold down the diagonal sections to create wings, about 1cm from the bottom line. Do this on both sides, comparing step 7 and step 8.

Step 8:
Your awesome flying paper airplane is all set for takeoff! Find a peaceful runway, like your house's terrace, and let it explore the skies!

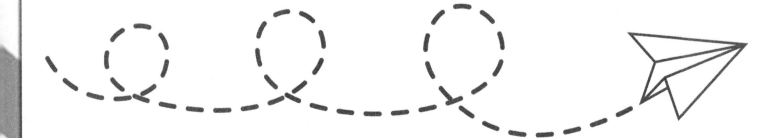

Let's Make The Bullseye

Did you know that narrow-winged planes fly faster, while long-winged planes glide gently and peacefully?

Introducing the Bullseye, a narrow-winged aircraft designed for speed and distance. With its sleek design, it can soar to faraway places with ease.

So, what are you waiting for? Lets make one!

Difficulty
★ ★ ★ ★ ★ 3.5

Cutting the Square:

Position your sheet vertically on the work table or floor, like a portrait rectangle. Grab the top right sharp edge and align it with the left side of the paper in a straight line. Now, using scissors, carefully cut off the remaining bottom piece of the paper.

Cut This Off

Step 1:

Start by placing the A4 sheet of paper in Portrait orientation on your work surface. Fold it from Left to Right equally, as shown. Once done, unfold it back to its original state.

Step 2:

Next, bring the Top Left-hand edge and Top Right-hand edge to the center crease. Be careful not to cross the center line.

Step 3:

Now, fold the right and left diagonal edges to the center crease, as illustratedhere. Once folded, unfold them back.

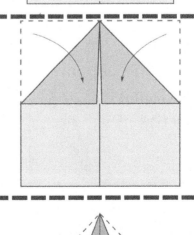

Bullseye

Step 4:
Fold the Right and left edges along the newly made crease, as shown here. Ensure that the edges are aligned with the adjacent crease.

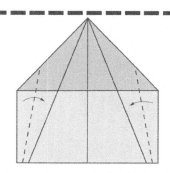

Step 5:
Roll fold the edges back inside, following the pattern!

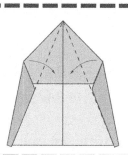

Step 6:
Refer to Fig.6 to determine the distance from the Nose to the bottom of the triangle. Divide this distance into three parts and fold down 1/3rd of the section.

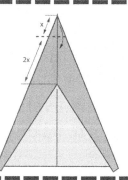

Step 7:
Mountain fold the paper airplane into half as indicated by the arrows.

Step 8:
Now, it's time to create the wings. Fold both sides down as shown.

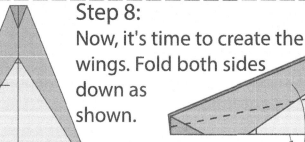

Step 9:
Lift the wings up to make them resemble a 'T'. You can refer to step 9 and step10 for guidance.

Step 10:
Your Bullseye paper airplane is now ready!

Let's Make The **CHARGER**

Difficulty

★ ★ ★ ★ ★ 1.5

You know, we all learn cool stuff from our parents, right? Like riding a bike or making paper airplanes! I learned how to make paper airplanes from my dad, just like you'll learn from this book. Making the best paper airplanes for kids is super fun and easy, especially when you have simple instructions to follow!

Step 1:
Get your A4 paper ready on a flat surface and fold it from left to right equally, like in the picture. Don't forget to unfold it afterward.

Step 2:
Next, bring the top-left and top-right edges of the paper down to meet the 1/3 mark of the middle line.

Step 3:
Fold the top-right and top-left edges down like triangles. It should look like the picture.

Step 4:
Now, fold the paper airplane in half along the center line and then unfold it. Then fold it in half again. You can see how in step 4 to step 5.

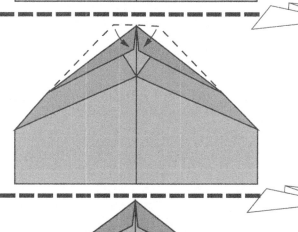

CHARGER

Step 5:
Now fold one side of the wings in half.

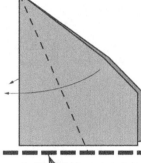

Step 6:
Repeat the same folding for the other side of the wings.

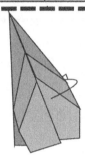

Step 7:
And there you have it! Your plane is ready to take off into the sky. Just give it a good toss and watch it soar high!

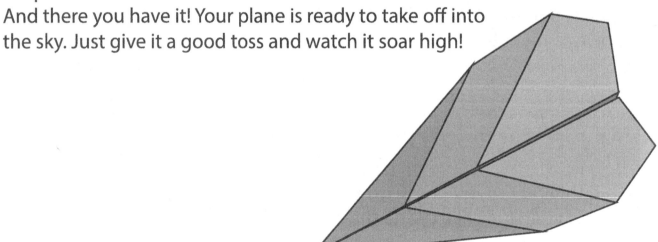

Let's Make The Cloud Breaker

In engineering, the angle between the two wings of a paper airplane is called dihedral. When the wings look like a 'Y' from the frontal view, it's dihedral; when they look like an 'A', it's anhedral. Paper airplanes with positive dihedral fly the best. Adding small pinches at the rear end of paper airplane designs creates elevators, which help the airplane ascend and descend. Elevators enable paper airplanes to fly higher and longer, while down elevators prevent stalling. The Cloud Breaker paper airplane, a sleek and high-speed design, knows how to swiftly navigate through the air currents.

Difficulty

★ ☆ ☆ ★ ★ 3.0

Step 1:
Get your sheet of paper and lay it down longways (portrait style) on a flat surface. Fold it in half from left to right and then unfold it back to its original position.

Step 2:
Now, take the top left corner and the top right corner and fold them down to meet in the middle. Make sure they don't go past the middle line.

Step 3:
Fold the top-left and top-right corners down to the center crease to make two diagonal lines. After folding, unfold them back to their original position.

Step 4:
Fold the edges on the right and left sides along the newly made crease. Make sure they align properly with the adjacent crease.

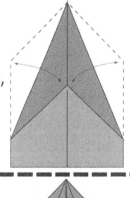
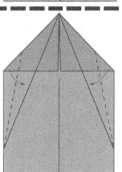

Cloud Breaker

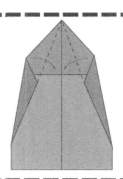

Step 5:
Now, fold those edges back inward, just like in the picture.

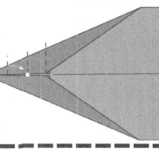

Step 6:
Measure the distance from the nose of the paper to the bottom of the triangle. Divide that distance into three parts and fold down one-third of the section from the top.

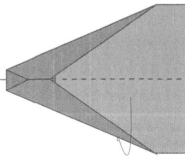

Step 7:
Fold the paper airplane in half along the center line, making sure it's symmetrical.

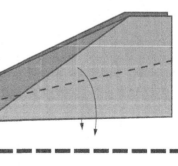

Step 8:
Time to make the wings! The length of the wings should match the length of the body. Fold the top diagonal section down to meet the bottom straight section, and do the same for the other side.

Step 9:
Lift the wings up so they're perpendicular to the body, forming a 'T' shape.

Step 10:
Hooray! Your Cloud Breaker paper airplane is all set for its grand debut. Let's have some fun!

Let's Make The Cloud Chaser

Difficulty

★ ★ ★ ★ ★ 4.0

The main goal in creating the best paper airplane for distance is to achieve greater flight lengths compared to a regular paper airplane. This same objective applies to creating the best paper airplane for speed. While only a few individuals may know the secrets to making the best paper airplane for distance and speed, how can everyone else learn to make one too?

Step 1:
First, fold the paper in half from left to right and then unfold it.

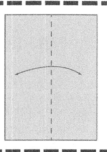

Step 2:
Now, fold down a small part of the top, about one-sixth of the paper, and match it with the center line.

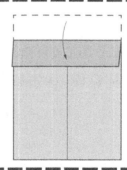

Step 3:
Fold the paper in half along the existing crease.

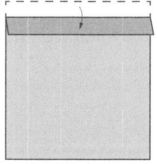

Step 4:
Do this one more time. Fold the top part down again, matching it with the center line.

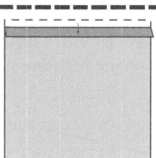

Cloud Chaser

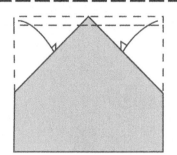

Step 5:
Next, fold the paper in half backwards along the center line.

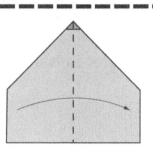

Step 6:
Fold the paper in half again, using the center line as a guide.

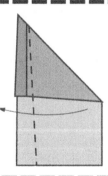

Step 7:
Now, fold the sections on one side to make the wings. Look at the picture for help.

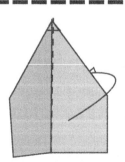

Step 8:
Repeat the same folding on the other side to make the other wing.

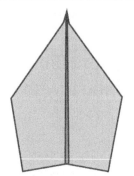

Step 9:
Congratulations! Now, it's time to fly! Find an open space for a great flight.

Let's Make The *Cloud Surfer*

Origami is a special way of making paper airplanes. The word "Origami" comes from Japan and means "folding papers." It's like a magic trick where you fold a piece of paper and turn it into something cool! Origami paper planes are a special type of paper airplane that you can make using this folding technique. Thanks to the clever folks from Japan, we have this awesome way to create amazing things out of paper. With origami, you can let your imagination soar!

Difficulty

★ ★ ★ ★ ★ 3.0

Step 1:
First, take your sheet of paper and fold it in half, then unfold it again. Next, bring the top edges of the paper to the center crease to make a cone shape.

Step 2:
Now, fold the diagonal edges on the left and right sides towards the center crease.

Step 3:
Fold the nose of the paper down so that it lines up with the straight line. Then, flip the paper over to the other side.

Step 4:
Follow the picture to the right and fold the paper as shown. Make sure the bottom of the fold is straight.

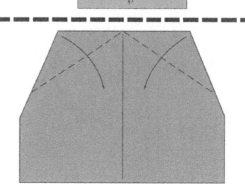

Cloud Surfer

Step 5:
Fold the nose of the paper using a mountain fold as shown. Sometimes, origami paper planes have a sharp nose design, which makes them a bit tricky to fold.

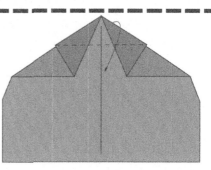

Step 6:
For the final fold, fold the paper along the center line, then make the wings by folding the paper as shown in step 6 and step 7.

Step 7:
Gently lift up the wings a bit, then launch your origami paper airplane into the air. Now, it's time to let your imagination soar as high as your paper airplane!

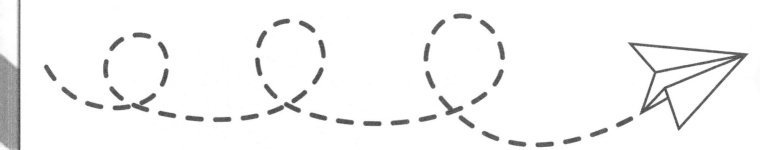

Let's Make The COMET CRASHER

In the this book, every paper airplane has its own special features and abilities. Some, like the darts, are easy to fold and fly. Yet, others require more careful attention to detail. But today, we're going to focus on creating our very best paper airplane, the Comet Crasher. Are you ready? Let's dive in and unleash our creativity!

Difficulty

★ ★ ★ ★ ★ 2.5

Step 1:

Place your sheet of paper flat on a table, making sure it's horizontal.

Step 2:

Fold the bottom edge up to meet the top edge, making a straight fold.

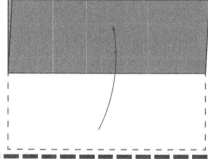

Step 3:

Fold the top-left and bottom-left corners towards the center crease, following the dotted lines like the picture shows.

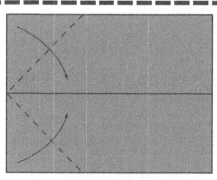

Step 4:

Fold along the dotted lines, making sure you fold about 3/4ths of the triangle.

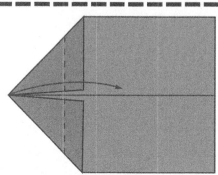

COMET CRASHER

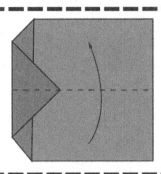

Step 5:
Fold the paper in half, ensuring both sides match up perfectly.

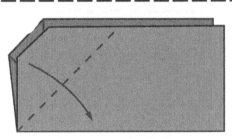

Step 6:
Fold down the top corner to the center fold, using the dotted line as a guide.

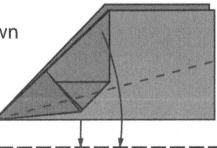

Step 7:
Now, let's make the wings! Fold both sides down just a bit below the main body of the plane.

Step 8:
Gently lift up the wings, as shown in in the picture to the right. Your Comet Crasher paper airplane is now ready to take flight!

Let's Make The Crimson Comet

Let's make a cool paper airplane called the Crimson Comet! Paper airplanes are awesome because you can fold them in different ways to make them fly really well. To make the Crimson Comet, we need to make special folds. Some folds go from edge to edge of the paper, and others go from edge to a crease. Every fold is important because it helps the airplane fly smoothly. Now, let's get started! Grab a piece of paper and follow along to make your very own Crimson Comet paper airplane!

Difficulty
★ ★ ★ ★ ★ 2.5

Step 1:
Take your sheet of paper and place it in landscape orientation. Fold it in half from top to bottom, making sure the edges meet perfectly. Then, unfold it.

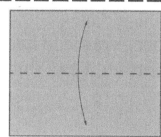

Step 2:
Now, fold the top left-hand edge down to meet the center crease like the picture shows.

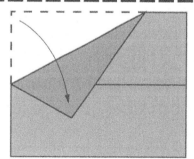

Step 3:
Next, fold the bottom left-hand edge up and overlap it on the previous fold.

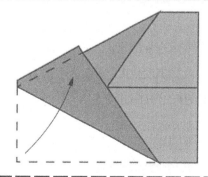

Step 4:
Fold the remaining flap on the edge from step 3. Your paper should look like step 4. Then, turn the paper over.

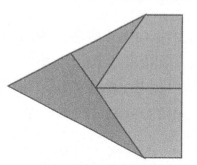

Crimson Comet

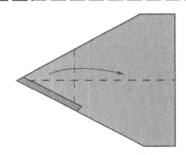

Step 5:
Fold down the nose of the airplane, making a triangle shape. Fold it down about 40% of the way, like the picture shows.

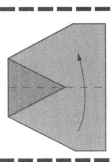

Step 6:
Fold your paper airplane in half, bringing the top down to meet the bottom. Make sure both sides look symmetrical.

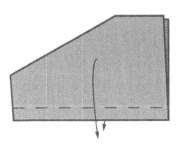

Step 7:
Fold down the diagonal sections to create wings. They should be about 1cm from the bottom edge. Do this on both sides, just like in step 7 and step 8.

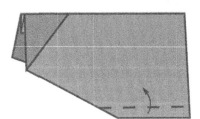

Step 8:
Now, let's make winglets! Fold the wings on both sides upward by about half an inch. This helps stabilize your airplane.

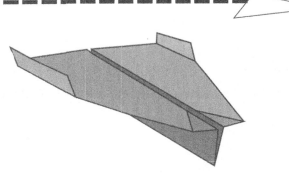

Step 9:
Your Crimson Comet Paper Airplane is now ready to fly! Take it outside and watch it soar through the air. Enjoy exploring the skies with your awesome paper creation!

Let's Make The DEAD SHOT

Difficulty

 ★ ★ ★ ★ ★ 2.0

Long ago, thousands of years ago, in China, someone made the very first paper airplane. But instead of soaring through the air, it ended up in the trash! Whose fault was that? Actually, it wasn't anyone's fault. We all have to learn how to make paper airplanes with the right shape and balance. So, let's make a cool paper airplane called Dead Shot now!

Step 1:
Place the sheet vertically on your table or flat, clean floor. Fold the top left (A) edge towards the right side edge and unfold. Repeat this with the top right section and unfold.

Step 2:
Fold the paper in half from top to bottom, using the dotted marks as a guide. Then, push both sides upwards where the arrows show, and the lower section will automatically meet the center.

Step 3:
Fold the outer edges of the top triangle to lie along the center crease. Fold both the right and left side edges of your Dead Shot design.

DEAD SHOT

Step 4:
Tuck the extra section inside the middle flap of your Dead Shot paper airplane.

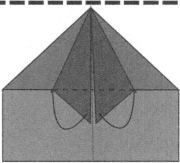

Step 5:
Fold the paper in half along the center crease line, creating a mountain fold.

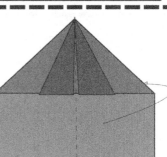

Step 6:
Fold the longer edges to the center line and line them up perfectly. Repeat on the other side of your Dead Shot paper airplane.

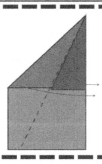

Step 7:
Gently lift up the wings slightly. Now, you're ready to fly high with your Dead Shot paper airplane!

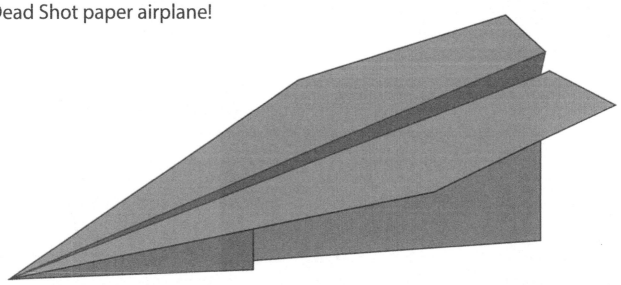

Let's Make The Dipper

You can learn all about the science behind paper airplane folding, flaps, and elevators. Imagine knowing how to make ten different paper airplanes! The next time you see someone struggling with their paper airplane, you can swoop in and help them out. You'll be like a paper airplane expert!

Difficulty

★ ★ ★ ★ ★ 3.0

Step 1:
Start by laying your paper flat on a table or surface, horizontally. Fold it in half from left to right, then unfold it.

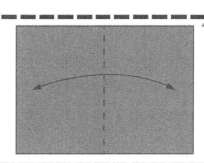

Step 2:
Now, bring the top-right and top-left corners to the center crease and fold them down.

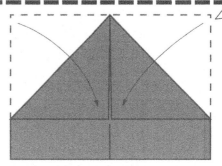

Step 3:
Fold the top part of the paper (the "nose") down to the bottom, aligning it with the center line.

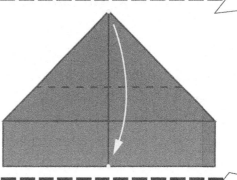

Step 4:
Fold the left half of the nose triangle to the center crease, matching the white lines.

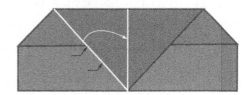

Dipper

Step 5:
Repeat the same fold for the right side. Your paper should now look like the picture.

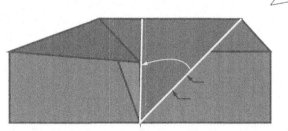

Step 6:
Carefully pull up the left side of the nose from the bottom of the front section, as shown. Be gentle and don't pull up too much.

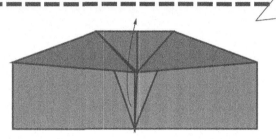

Step 7:
Fold the paper in half along the center crease and check that both sides are symmetrical.

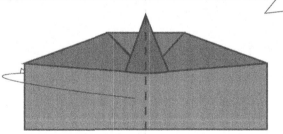

Step 8:
Now, fold the wings diagonally, referring to the fuselage. Do this on both sides to create the wings.

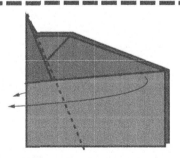

Step 9:
Your paper airplane is ready to fly! Find a good spot, like an open ground or school auditorium, and let it soar through the air peacefully. Enjoy

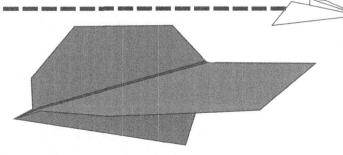

Let's Make The *Flight Fury*

Difficulty

★★★★★ 2.5

Long, long ago, in a land far away called China, people discovered something amazing: paper! Yes, the very thing we use every day to write, draw, and even make paper airplanes! Can you imagine a world without paper?

Well, the clever folks in China figured out how to make paper, and they came up with all sorts of fun things to do with it. One of the most popular activities was folding paper into airplanes and sending them soaring into the sky!

Step 1:

Let's start by placing your paper on the table with its long side up. Fold it in half from right to left, then gently unfold it.

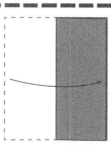

Step 2:

Now, we're going to fold the top left corner, marked as A, towards the center crease. Make sure it lines up perfectly with the center line and the left boundary line.

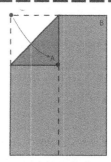

Step 3:

Next, take the top right-hand edge, marked as B, and fold it towards the center, just like we did with corner A.

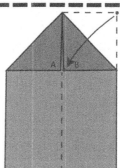

Step 4:

Fold corner C over to meet the center line, and then do the same with corner D. When you're done, your paper should look like the shape in this picture.

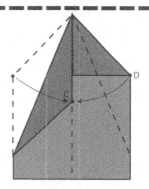

Flight Fury

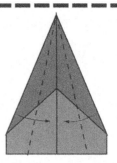

Step 5:
Now, fold the left and right side sections towards the center line. Be careful not to go over the center line!

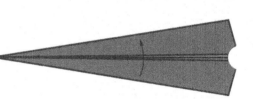

Step 6:
Fold your paper jet in half along the center crease, and give it a good crease.

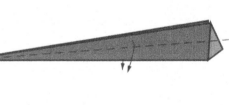

Step 7:
It's time to make the wings! Separate the wings and fold them down. You can follow along with the pictures in step 6, step 7, and step 8.

Step 8:
Now, let's add some winglets! Make small folds on the edges of the wings, just like in this.

Step 9:
Finally, gently lift both sides of the wings to give them some extra lift. And there you have it – your paper jet is ready to take off into the sky!

Let's Make The *Flighty Feather*

The secret to making amazing paper airplanes is in their front part. Some paper airplanes barely fly even a short distance because they're not made properly. To make the best paper airplane, you need to make sure the front part is heavier. This helps the airplane fly straight when you throw it. Flighty Feather has a special design with extra weight in the front, which helps it fly even better, especially in strong winds.

Difficulty

★ ★ ★ ★ ★ 2.5

Step 1:

Start by placing your paper in portrait orientation on the table. Fold it in half from left to right, then unfold it. Now, fold it in half from top to bottom, and unfold it again, just like shown.

Step 2:

Fold the top section of the paper down to the center crease you just made in step 1. Match the white dots with the guide arrow to make sure it's centered.

Step 3:

Fold the top section down again, this time using the central horizontal crease as the center reference point.

Step 4:

Bring the top right-hand edge and the top left-hand edge to the center line, making sure the white dots meet at the center.

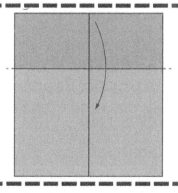
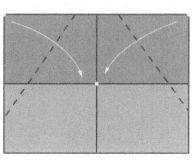

Flighty Feather

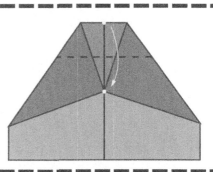

Step 5:
Fold the nose section down to half of its length, matching the dots as shown here.

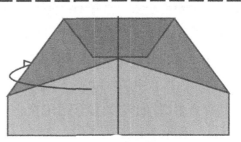

Step 6:
Now, fold the plane in half along the central crease to the back section. Check to make sure both halves are symmetrical.

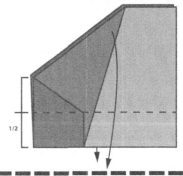

Step 7:
Fold the wings down, making them half the length of the frontal section.

1/2

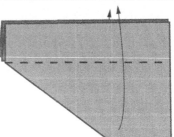

Step 8:
Now, fold the diagonal section up, lifting it entirely to the upside. Repeat the same for the other side.

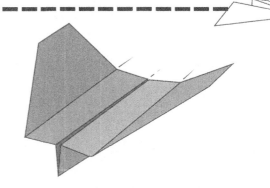

Step 9:
Congratulations! You've successfully made a fighter plane. It flies well and smoothly, especially with gentle launches.

Let's Make The *Flinger*

Difficulty
★ ★ ★ ★ ★ 1.5

Did you know that making origami paper planes is like studying real airplanes? It's true! Paper planes are not just fun toys, they're also a great way to learn about science and technology.

Learning about paper planes can be a super cool part of STEM education. It's a chance for kids to dive into the world of aviation studies and learn how airplanes work.

Step 1:
First, lay your sheet of paper flat on the table with the long sides on the top and bottom. Fold the paper in half from left to right, then unfold it.

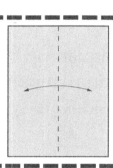

Step 2:
Now, fold the top left corner and the top right corner down to meet the center crease line. Be careful not to cross the center line when folding.

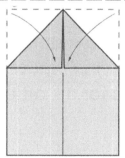

Step 3:
Fold the top of the paper down to meet the bottom edge, creating a triangle shape. Make sure the height of the triangle matches the distance from the bottom of the triangle to the straight line you've folded.

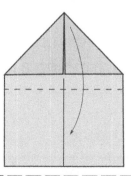

Step 4:
Fold the top left and top right edges down to meet the center crease line again, without crossing it.

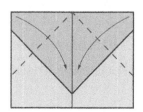

Flinger

Step 5:
Fold up the small triangle at the bottom of the big triangle, as shown in here.

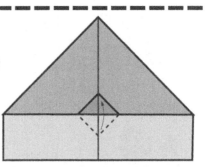

Step 6:
Fold the paper airplane in half along the center crease line, creating a mountain fold. Check to make sure both sides are symmetrical.

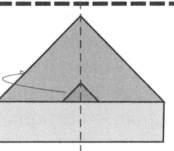

Step 7:
Fold the wings down along the fuselage, leaving about 1 cm of space to hold onto. Repeat this step for the other side of the plane.

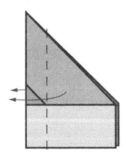

Step 8:
Gently lift the wings up so they are perpendicular to the fuselage, forming a 'T' shape.

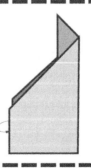

Step 9:
Congratulations! You've made a flying paper airplane! It performs well and flies smoothly, especially with gentle launches. Have fun flying it!

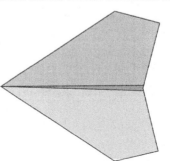

Let's Make The Folded Falcon

Difficulty

★ ★ ★ ★ ★ 1.5

When you throw a paper airplane, its special shape helps it create lift. Lift is a force that pushes up on the airplane, kind of like a magic wind that keeps it in the air. But why does the paper airplane make lift and not the crumpled paper?

That's because the paper airplane is carefully folded to have wings, just like a real airplane. These wings are curved on top and flat on the bottom. When you throw the paper airplane, air rushes over the curved top of the wings faster than the air goes under the wings.

Step 1:
Start by placing your sheet of paper on the table in portrait orientation. Fold it in half from right to left, then unfold it.

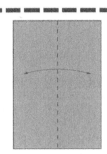

Step 2:
Fold the top right and left corners of the paper towards the center crease. Be careful not to cross the center line.

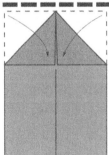

Step 3:
Now, fold the right and left diagonal edges towards the center crease as shown.

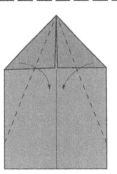

Step 4:
Fold the nose of the airplane down along the dotted lines, aligning the center of the fold with the white dots.

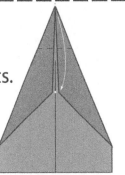

Folded Falcon

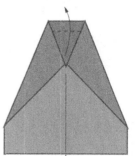

Step 5:
Gently push the nose of the airplane up by folding it about 1cm as shown.

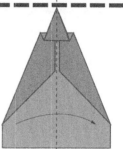

Step 6:
Fold the plane in half by bringing the left end to meet the right end. Make sure they match perfectly and check for symmetry.

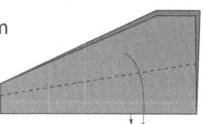

Step 7:
Fold the wings down along the dotted lines to form the wings of the airplane. Do this on both sides, using the dotted lines as guides.

Step 8:
Lift up the wings to give them a "T" shape when viewed from the front.

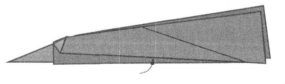

Step 9:
Your Folded Falcon paper airplane is now ready for takeoff! Have fun flying it through the sky!

Let's Make The Folded Fury

Difficulty

★ ★ ★ ★ ★ 1.5

In the world of aerodynamics, there are four main forces at play when an object, like a paper airplane, takes flight. These forces are lift, weight (gravity), thrust, and drag. Among these, gravity plays a crucial role. Gravity is what keeps us grounded on Earth, and it also affects how objects move through the air. If there were no gravity (weight), paper airplanes wouldn't be able to fly properly. Here's why:

Gravity provides the necessary downward force that keeps the paper airplane balanced and stable in the air.

Step 1:
Start by laying your paper flat on the table or floor. Fold it in half from left to right, then unfold it.

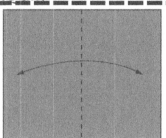

Step 2:
Now, bring the top right and left corners to the center crease and fold them down.

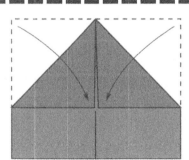

Step 3:
Next, fold the diagonal edges on both sides to meet at the center crease, like shown.

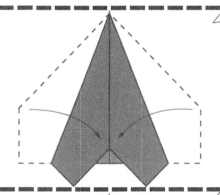

Step 4:
Fold the paper airplane in half from left to right, making sure both sides match up evenly.

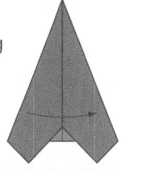

Folded Fury

Step 5:
Fold the wings down on both sides, about 1cm from the bottom, to create the Fury's wings.

Step 6:
To add stability, fold the wings upward on]both sides to create winglets. This helps keep your aircraft steady during flight. Compare step 6 and 7 for guidance.

Step 7:
Your paper airplane is now ready to take flight! Get ready to soar high in the sky and conquer the clouds!

Let's Make The Gale Sail

Difficulty

★★★★⯪ 4.5

Before we start making this new paper airplane design, let's learn something interesting! Did you know that every paper airplane is unique and has its own special features? But here's the fun part: when you make a paper plane, you need to fly it many times to see how it behaves. Pay attention to how it flies and any problems it might have. Then, you can figure out what to do next! By studying its aerodynamics and making small tweaks and adjustments, you can make your paper airplane fly even better!

Step 1:

First, let's cut off one-quarter of the paper's width. If you're not sure how to do this, don't worry! Just fold the paper in half, and then fold the folded half in half again. When you unfold it, you'll see the quarter space. Now, trim it off!

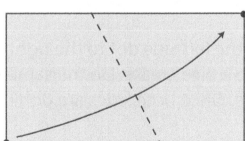

Step 2:

Now, place the paper in landscape mode on the table or floor. Take the bottom left corner and fold it up to meet the top right corner.

Step 3:

Look closely at the picture to the right. You'll see two dots at the top. Fold the paper along the dotted lines so that these dots meet at the center. Once you've done that, unfold the paper.

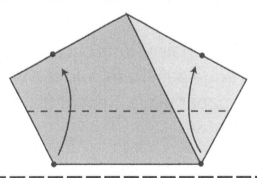

Step 4:

Fold the bottom edge of the paper up to the crease you just made in Step 3. This will create a new crease.

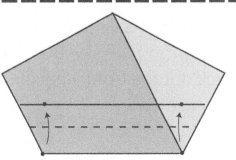

Step 5:
Now, fold and roll over the paper to complete Step 4 and then repeat Step 3.

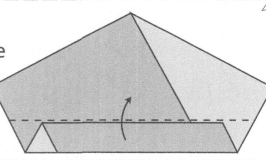

Step 6:
Fold the paper in half along the center crease, just like shown.

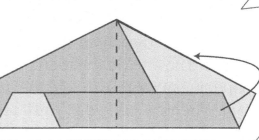

Step 7:
Connect the left side dot to the right side dot and make a nice crease. Do the same for the other side. Once both sides are done, unfold them.

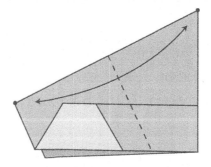

Step 8:
Fold the middle pair of dots over to meet the top right-hand edge pair. Then, fold the winglet at the edge of the paper plane. Repeat the same steps for the other side.

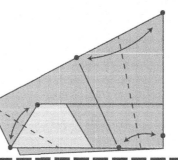

Step 9:
Congratulations! Your Gale Sail paper airplane is now ready to soar to new heights in the sky! But before you launch it, don't forget to check out the front view of the plane shown below.

FRONT VIEW

Let's Make The GLIDE GUARDIAN

Difficulty
★ ★ ★ ★ ★ 1.5

Just like we've talked about in our previous paper airplane tutorials, aircraft experience four main forces: lift, weight, thrust, and drag. When you throw a paper plane, your throw gives it lift, while the air trying to slow it down is drag. The mass of the paper airplane is its weight (gravity), and the wings provide an upward force called lift. The design of the wings helps provide a good amount of lift consistently with every throw.

Step 1:
Start with your paper in portrait mode, then fold it evenly from left to right as shown here. After folding, unfold it again.

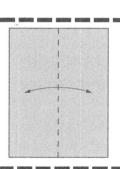

Step 2:
Bring the top edges of the paper to the center crease, making sure not to cross the center line.

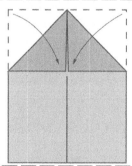

Step 3:
Fold the nose of the paper down to a straight line. Compare the height of the folded nose to the triangle below it to ensure they match, as shown in step 3 and step 4.

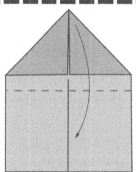

Step 4:
Fold the top edges of the paper to the center crease, covering about 3/4 of its length. Check the picture to see where they should meet.

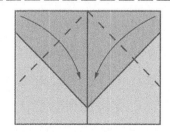

GLIDE GUARDIAN

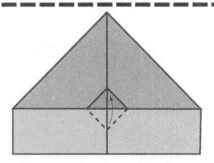

Step 5:
Pull up the nose of your airplane and lock it in place using the technique shown here.
This will keep your airplane steady during flight.

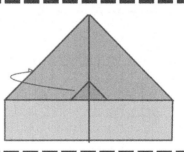

Step 6:
Now, fold your Guardian paper airplane in half along the center crease, making sure it's symmetrical.

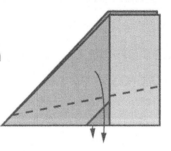

Step 7:
It's time to add wings! Fold about an inch from the bottom of your airplane diagonally to create wings. The dotted lines will guide you. Repeat the process on the other side.

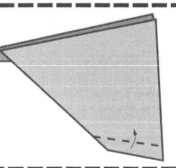

Step 8:
For extra stability, let's make some winglets! Fold the edges of the wings upwards by about half an inch to create winglets.

Step 9:
Congratulations! Your Aloft Craft Levitator paper airplane is now ready for takeoff! Find a nice spot, launch it gently, and watch it soar through the skies. Have fun exploring the skies with your amazing creation!

Let's Make The Leaf Jet

Did you know that many amazing inventions started with something as simple as paper? It's true! Just think about it: Einstein's theory of relativity, Graham Bell's telephone, and even the first flying airplane by the Wright brothers all had their beginnings in simple paper creations.

Airplanes have certainly come a long way since those early days, but you know what's cool? You can start your own journey right here with paper airplanes!

Difficulty

★ ☆ ☆ ☆ ☆ 5.0

Step 1:
Place your sheet on the table in portrait mode. Fold it in half from right to left, then unfold it. This will be the starting point for your airplane.

Step 2:
Now, fold the right edge of the paper straight to the center, and do the same for the left side. Make sure to crease the folds firmly.

Step 3:
Next, fold the top right corner of the paper to the center line, and then fold the top left corner to the center line too. This will create a triangle shape.

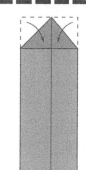

Step 4:
Now, fold the rectangles below the triangle outward until they reach their limit lines.

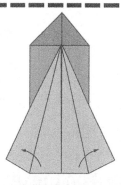

Leaf Jet

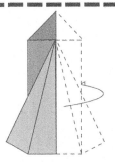

Step 5:
Fold the paper airplane in half towards the backside, making sure the center line doesn't cross. Then, unfold it.

Step 6:
About 1 to 1.5cm below the triangle, fold the paper downwards and make a crease.

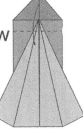

Step 7:
Now, fold the nose of the plane upwards (mountain fold) as shown. Then unfold it. If you're having trouble, go back to Step 1 and try again!

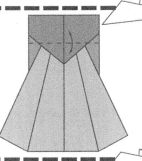

Step 8:
Fold the top right corner and the top left corner to the center line. Make sure to crease the folds firmly.

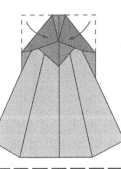

Step 9:
Fold the pointed nose upwards (mountain fold) so the tip meets the straight center line. This will give your airplane its final shape.

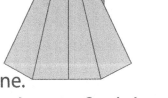

Step 10:
Fold the airplane in half towards the backside, ensuring that both halves are similar to each other.

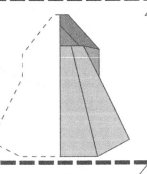

Step 11:
Now, check for the lines indicating where to fold the nose angle change and tail angle change. Fold them as shown in the picture. Repeat on the other side.

Step 12:
Your paper airplane is all set to fly! Take it outside and let it soar through the sky.

Let's Make The LONG SHOT

Difficulty

★★★★★ 2.0

Did you know that the largest paper airplane ever made was created by students and employees at the Braunschweig Institute of Technology in Germany? It's true!
This gigantic paper airplane was launched in an aircraft hangar from a platform that was 8.10 feet (2.47 meters) high. And guess what? It flew a whopping distance of just over 59 feet (18 meters)!
But wait, there's more! This incredible paper airplane wasn't just big, it was also made entirely out of paper. Can you believe it?

Step 1:
First, lay your paper flat on the table or floor in a horizontal position. Fold it in half from left to right, then unfold it.

Step 2:
Next, bring the top right-hand edge and the top left-hand edge to the center crease and fold them.

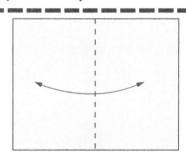

Step 3:
Now, fold the right and left diagonal edges to the center crease as shown. Once you're done, unfold them.

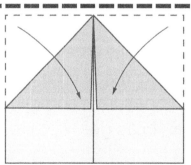

Step 4:
Fold the right and left sides of the paper to the creases you made in the previous step.

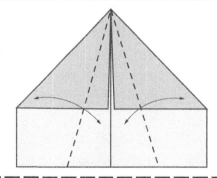

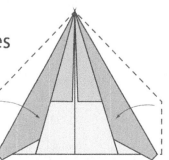

LONG SHOT

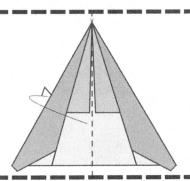

Step 5:
Fold your paper airplane in half along the center crease, but this time fold it towards the backside.

Step 6:
Fold the wings from the right to the left, matching the diagonal right section to the straight left section.

Step 7:
Lift up the wings so they look like a 'T'. Your paper airplane is now ready for a good range flight! Head to an open area and give it a throw to see how far it can go!

Have fun flying your paper airplane designs and see how far you can make them soar!

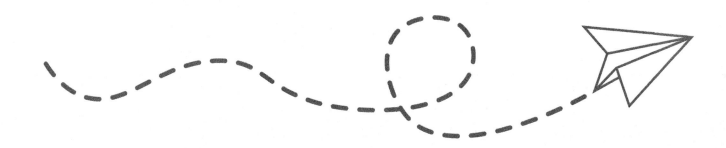

Let's Make The MIGHTY FLIGHT

Hold on a sec, why are we talking about failing? Well, let me tell you, there's a good reason for it! Sometimes, the best paper airplane designs come after a bunch of tries and, yes, even some fails. It's all part of the fun and learning!

To make a really awesome paper airplane, you gotta experiment with different techniques and folds. That's how you'll discover the ones that make your plane fly super high and far!

Difficulty
★★★★☆ 4.5

Step 1:
First things first, lay your paper flat on the table in a horizontal position. Now, fold it in half along the center line, creating a valley fold.

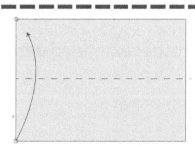

Step 2:
Fold the sections as shown making sure not to cross the center crease. Be careful, buddy!

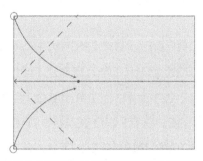

Step 3:
Now, flip your paper over to the backside. Make two valley folds just like in the picture.

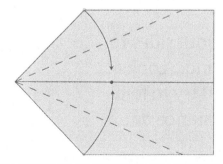

Step 4:
You'll see an extended dragon-like section on the top. Don't worry, that's supposed to happen! Fold the two sections to the center line.

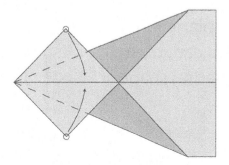

MIGHTY FLIGHT

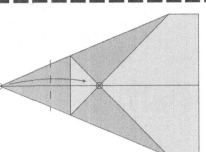

Step 5:
Fold the top sharp edge, marked by a circle, to the center dot. Just follow where the arrow points.

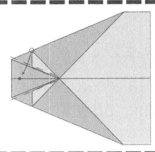

Step 6:
Now, fold the other extended area to the center dot.

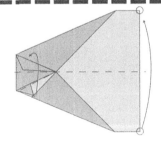

Step 7:
This step might be a bit tricky. If you're a kid like me, you can ask your mom for help. Fold the rounded edge and insert it into the other side's socket. You'll need to close the model to do this, so fold the whole plane to the center line and try to insert it on the other side.

Step 8:
Valley fold both sides to make the wings. Look at the lines and try to fold the same distance on both sides.

Step 9:
Now, let's make the winglets! Fold both sides as shown and straighten them to 90 degrees. These will help stabilize your flight.

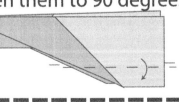

Step 10:
Reform the plane into a 'T' shape. If you can, try to give it a dihedral shape too.

Step 11:
Actually, there's no Step 11, my friend! Just sit back, relax, and have fun!

Let's Make The Nakamura Lock Dart

Nakamura Dart got its name from a talented Japanese Origami artist who created it. This plane is special because its weight is spread out evenly, making it fly better when you launch it. The Nakamura lock paper airplane combines elements of both dart and glider planes. Give it a gentle throw, and it won't let you down! One of its coolest features is the Origami lock that keeps it sturdy for many flights.

Difficulty

★ ★ ★ ★ ★ 0.0

Step 1:

Get a sheet of paper and hold it upright, like a portrait. Fold the paper in half from top to bottom, making a mountain fold. Make sure the fold reaches the center line on both sides. If it looks like a house, you're doing it right!

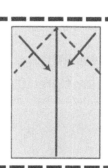

Step 2:

Fold the top sharp edge down to the bottom edge. Press firmly to make a crisp fold.

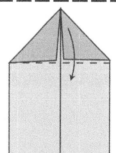

Step 3:

Fold the top right and left corners down to about 3/4 of the way to the center line from the top. Paper Plane Fun Fact: The Nakamura dart is one of the best flying dart paper planes and can glide really well!

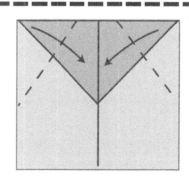

Step 4:

Make sure both sides are aligned perfectly with the center line. Fold the bottom part up towards the top, just like in the next picture (Step 5)

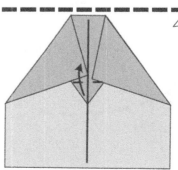

Nakamura Lock Dart

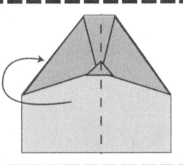

Step 5:
Now, fold the paper in half along the center dotted line towards the back. You're almost there!

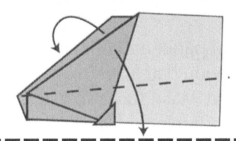

Step 6:
Fold down the wings, using the dotted lines as guides. Make sure your folds are strong and neat.

Step 7:
You're all set to take flight! Congratulations, you've made a fantastic Nakamura lock paper airplane!

Let's Make The Nimbus Nester

Paper airplanes are super cool because they have a special point called the center of gravity. It's like the balancing point of their wings. If you can balance a paper airplane on one finger, you've found its center of gravity! But did you know that the shape of the airplane can change where this point is?

Difficulty

★★★★★ 5.0

Now, let's learn how to make the tough Nimbus Nester paper airplane.

Step 1:

First, lay your paper flat on a table or any smooth surface with the long edges at the top and bottom. Fold it in half from left to right, then unfold it.

Step 2:

Now, bring the top right-hand corner and the top left-hand corner down to meet the center crease. Fold them neatly.

Step 3:

Fold the top of the paper, which is called the nose, down to the bottom edge, making sure it aligns with the center crease. This creates a triangle shape. Imagine connecting the white dots to make this fold!

Step 4:

Take the top right-hand corner and the left-hand corner and fold them down to meet the folded nose at the bottom. Compare Step 4 and 5 to help you!

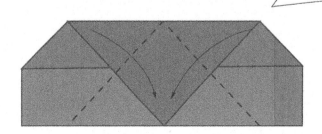

Nimbus Nester

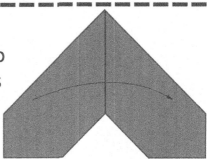

Step 5:
Fold your paper airplane in half, bringing the top down to meet the bottom. Make sure both sides look the same to get a symmetrical airplane.

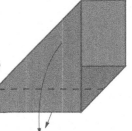

Step 6:
Turn your paper airplane sideways, like in the picture. Fold the wings down so they're about 1 cm above the body of the airplane on both sides.

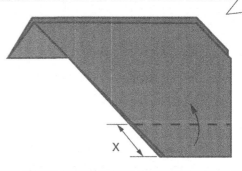

Step 7:
Now, let's make some winglets! Fold the sides of the wings up, matching the height of the fuselage (that's the body of the airplane). Do this on both sides.

Step 8:
Your awesome paper airplane is now ready for an epic flight! Give it a giant leap and watch it soar through the air.

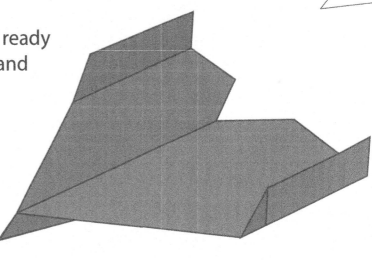

Let's Make
The RAPID ROCKET

Difficulty
⭐⭐⭐⭐⭐ 1.0

When you first try to fly a paper airplane, it might not go very far. But if you fold it tightly and make sharp creases, it will perform better! Things like making sure it's symmetrical and accurate with your folds also make a big difference. Some planes might take a bit longer to make and can be a little frustrating, but they're worth it! As you practice and get better, you'll be able to show off your awesome paper airplane skills to your friends and family!

Step 1:
Place the A4 sheet horizontally on a table or flat surface.
Fold it in half vertically like a hot dog bun, then unfold it as shown in the picture.

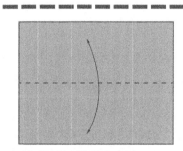

Step 2:
Next, fold the top right corner and the bottom right corner edges towards the center crease.
Fold along the dotted lines in the direction of the arrow, as shown in the picture.

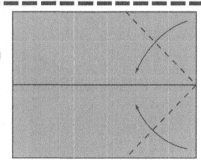

Step 3:

Now, fold the paper in half from bottom to top, like closing a book, as shown in the picture.

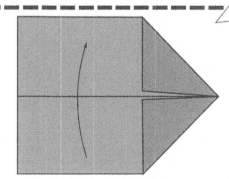

Step 4:
Fold the corners on the right side of both sections down towards the bottom straight line. Make sure to fold them slightly below halfway down the length of the paper and above the bottom line. If you're unsure, you can look at the picture in step 5 for help.

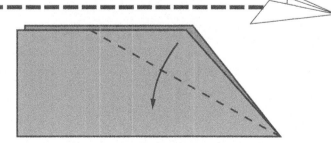

RAPID ROCKET

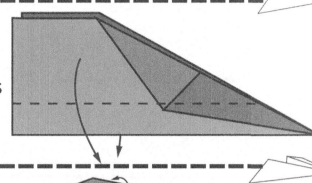

Step 5:
Now it's time to make the wings of the Rapid Rocket paper airplane. Follow the dotted lines in the center and fold them down as shown.

Step 6:
Create the winglets using the dotted guidelines to make them straight and equal. Then, fold the winglets upward on both sides of the wing.

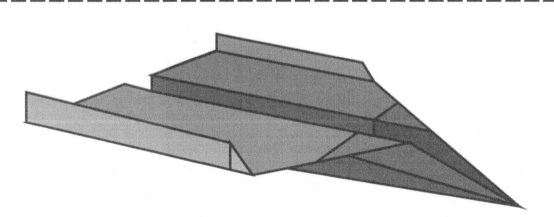

Step 7:

Gently lift the wings upward to make them look like a 'T'. Also, make sure to adjust the winglets vertically straight to achieve a better flight,

Let's Make The  SKY CRUISER

Difficulty

★★★★★ 2.0

Making a paper airplane is just the beginning of the adventure! Before you launch it into the sky, there are some important checks and tweaks you need to do. Even the best-designed paper airplane won't fly properly if it's not straight. So, let's make sure everything is aligned perfectly.

First, check the alignment of your paper airplane. Make sure the wings, winglets, fin, and tail are all aligned, flat, and straight. If they're not, gently tweak them until they are.

Step 1:
Place your paper flat on the table, with the long sides on the top and bottom. Fold it in half from left to right, then unfold it.

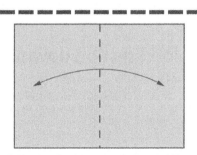

Step 2:
Take the top corners on the right and left sides and fold them down to meet the center crease.

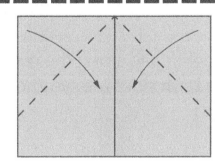

Step 3:
Bring the top edge of the paper down to the bottom edge, creating a fold in the middle. Then unfold it.

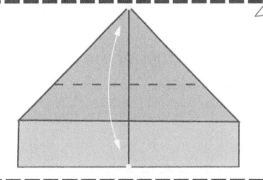

Step 4:
Fold the top point of the paper down to the crease you made in Step 3.

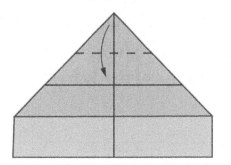

Step 5:
Fold the small triangle at the bottom in half, dividing it into two equal parts.

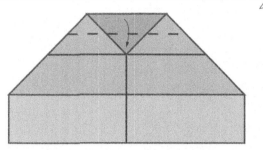

Step 6:
Roll the top folded section downwards, as shown.

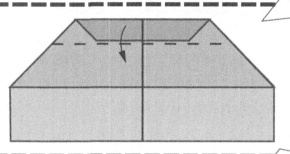

Step 7:
Fold the paper in half along the center crease, making sure both sides are symmetrical.

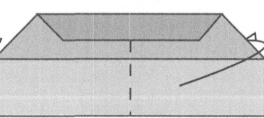

Step 8:
Fold the bottom edges of the paper up to create wings on both sides.

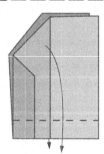

Step 9:
Now, find a good spot to launch your Sky Cruiser paper airplane—like an open area or a school auditorium. Then, get ready to fly!

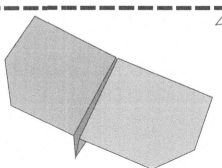

Let's Make The Sky Pepper

Difficulty

⭐⭐⭐⭐⭐ 2.5

Just like real airplanes, paper airplanes also have control surfaces that help them move around in the air. These control surfaces are like secret buttons that make the plane do different tricks and moves. But be careful! If these control surfaces get messed up, your plane might not fly as well.

Today, we're going to make a special paper airplane called the Sky Pepper. It's not just any ordinary paper airplane; it's got some awesome control surfaces that make it do amazing things in the air.

Step 1:

Lay your sheet vertically on your table or floor, just like a tall rectangle.
Fold the top right corner down to meet the left side of the paper, making a nice sharp edge.

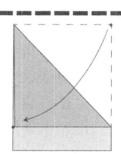

Step 2:

Now, it's time to trim off the bottom piece of the paper with some scissors. Make sure to follow along carefully, or else your plane might not turn out quite right. Check out the picture for a visual guide on where to cut.

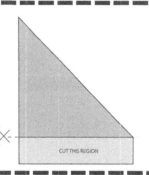

CUT THIS REGION

Step 3:

Fold your square sheet in half from top to bottom, and then unfold it. Next, fold the section labeled "A" to the center crease you just made, and then unfold it again.

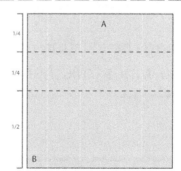

Step 4:

Pay close attention to this step! Take the bottom left corner labeled "B" (from step 3) and fold it up to the upper crease, but make sure you don't cross the center crease. Got it? Now, let's move on to the next step.

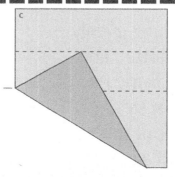

Sky Pepper

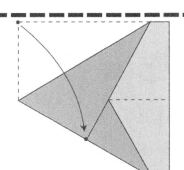

Step 5:
Now, bring the top left corner labeled "C" (step 4) down to meet the dot-to-dot line, following the direction of the arrow in the picture.

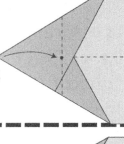

Step 6:
Fold the nose of your Sky Pepper plane down to meet the dotted line. If you're not sure where that line should be, take a good look at picture for a few seconds to understand the distance from the nose.

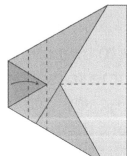

Step 7:
Feeling happy with your progress? Great! Let's fold the plane once more along the bottom line, just like shown.

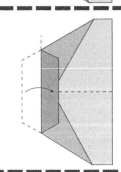

Step 8:
Now, fold along the existing crease one more time. Then, fold the wings together on the backside, like shown to the right?

Step 9:
Fold the plane evenly along the dotted line. Repeat the same fold for the other side. Awesome job! You've got yourself a plane!

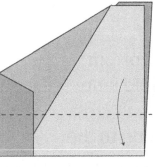

Step 10:
Gently lift up the wings, and you're all set for a flying adventure!

Let's Make The SKY SHAPER

In real airplanes, the wings are angled slightly upwards. This tilt helps create higher pressure beneath the wings, giving the airplane lift. The more the wings are tilted, the more lift they generate. However, if the wings tilt too much, beyond a critical angle, the airplane may slow down or stall, creating drag.
When you launch a paper airplane, the angle and position at which you launch it are crucial for a successful flight.

Difficulty

★ ★ ★ ★ ★ **3.5**

Step 1:
First, lay your paper flat on the table. Fold it in half from left to right, then unfold it.

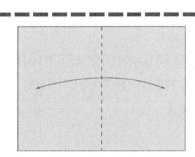

Step 2:
Next, fold the top corners down to the center crease to make a triangle shape.

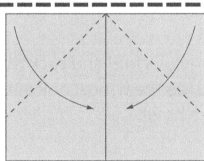

Step 3:
Now, lift up the flaps on both sides and match the diagonal edges together.

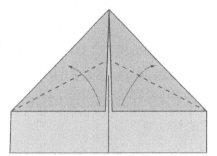

Step 4:
Fold the top point (the nose) down to where it meets the remaining paper at the top.

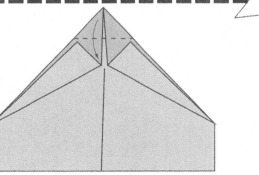

SKY SHAPER

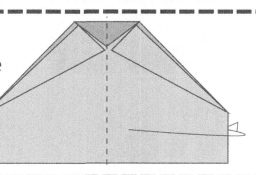

Step 5:
Fold the paper in half along the center crease and make sure both sides are symmetrical.

Step 6:
Fold the bottom straight section up to match the diagonal bottom of the wings. Look at the pictures for help!

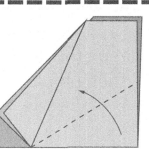

Step 7:
Unfold the previous fold and tuck the section you folded inside the wing. Look at the pictures to see how!

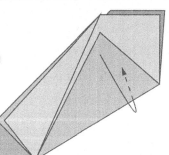

Step 8:
Fold down the wings along the dotted lines. Each side should have two sections, with the left side divided into thirds and the right side folded to the bottom.

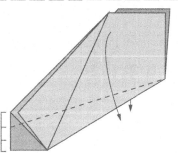

Step 9:
Fold the fin in half and tuck it inside.

Step 10:
Your Sky Shaper paper airplane is ready to fly!

Let's Make The

SKY STRIKE

Difficulty

★ ★ ★ ★ ★ 0.0

Now, let me tell you about a special paper airplane called the Sky Strike. It's designed to do all sorts of cool things and it's one of the best paper airplanes out there. It's like a glider, which means it can soar through the air gracefully. How cool is that? Let's make one and see how it flies!

Step 1:

Let's start by making the center crease of our soaring paper airplane. Fold the paper from top to bottom evenly and crease it well. Now, fold corner A so it meets the center line without crossing it. Make a nice, firm crease. Do the same with corner B, but on the opposite side.

Step 2:

Flip your paper airplane over. Fold the top part back about 3 to 4 centimeters. Then, make a mountain fold along the center crease in the direction of the arrow. This will give your airplane its soaring shape!

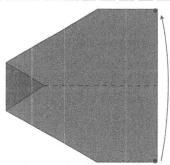

Step 3:

Now, fold the paper airplane along the dotted line evenly on both sides. Make sure to do the same for both sides of the airplane.

Step 4:

Here comes the fun part! Let's make some wings for our plane. Fold the winglets as shown.

Step 5:

Lift up the wings of your paper airplane. If you look from the rear, you should see a 'T' or 'Y' shape. That means your airplane is ready to fly! Get ready to launch it and watch it soar through the sky!

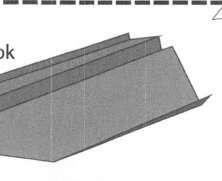

When I was a kid, my friends and I loved making paper airplanes. We would spend hours folding them just right, trying out different designs to see which one could fly the farthest. One sunny afternoon, we decided to have a paper airplane contest at the park.

I folded my plane carefully, making sure the wings were just the right size and the nose was pointed just so. With a flick of my wrist, I launched it into the air, watching with excitement as it soared through the sky. But then, disaster struck – a sudden gust of wind caught my plane and sent it spiraling off course.

Before I knew it, my paper airplane was stuck high up in a tree, its wings caught on a branch. I tried to reach it with a stick, jumping and stretching as high as I could, but it was no use. My plane was stuck, and there was nothing I could do to get it down.

I felt frustrated and disappointed as I watched my friends' planes continue to fly through the air, looping and gliding gracefully. But then I realized something – even though my plane was stuck in the tree, I had still had a lot of fun making it and watching it fly, if only for a moment.

So, I decided to let go of my frustration and enjoy the rest of the afternoon with my friends. And who knows? Maybe someday, when the wind blows just right, my paper airplane will come sailing back down to earth, ready for another flight. But until then, I'll always remember the day I got my paper airplane stuck in a tree – a silly mishap that turned into a cherished childhood memory.

Let's Make The Sky Surfer

Did you know there are world records for paper airplanes? Yup, it's true! And they look at two important things: how far a plane can fly (that's called maximum range) and how long it can stay in the air (that's called maximum endurance).

Before you try to break a world record with your paper airplane, it's a good idea to learn more about it.

Difficulty

 0.5

Step 1:
Place your sheet of paper in portrait orientation on a table or flat surface. Fold the right-hand end over to the left side and match it up, just like in the picture to the right.

Step 2:
Now, let's tackle the left-hand side! Fold the top edge of the left side over to meet the end of the triangle on the right side.

Step 3:
Time to give our plane a nose! Fold the front of the paper airplane down to the bottom of the triangle along the dotted lines.

Step 4:
Fold the paper airplane in half from left to right, making sure both sides match up perfectly. Symmetry is key!

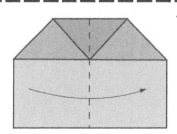

Sky Surfer

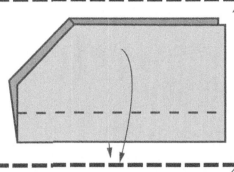

Step 5:
Fold the wings down on both sides, about 1.5cm from the bottom.

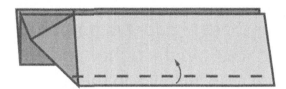

Step 6:
Let's add some winglets for stability! Fold the wings on both sides upward by about half an inch.

Step 7:
This paper airplane believes in its wings! It's had some great performances in strong winds. Now, let's give it a test flight and see how it soars!

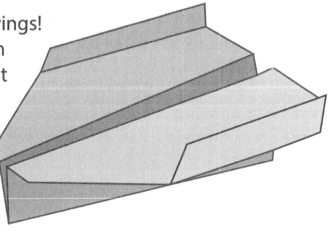

Let's Make The SLICK SLIDER

Difficulty

★ ★ ★ ★ ★ 2.5

Did you know that Orville and Wilbur Wright, two awesome inventors, made a small version of their airplane to test how it flies? Pretty cool, right? That means anyone, whether you're a kid or a grown-up, can start making your very own paper airplanes too!

Let's talk about the Slick Slider. It's got a super easy design and simple instructions, so you can fold it up in just a few minutes and start enjoying flying it around.

So, are you ready? Let's do this!

Step 1:

First, place your sheet vertically on your work table or the floor. Fold the top right corner over to match the left side of the paper neatly.

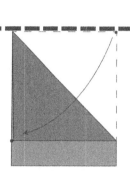

Step 2:

Now, it's time to trim off the bottom piece of the paper with some scissors. Make sure to follow along carefully, or else your plane might not turn out quite right. Check out the picture for a visual guide on where to cut.

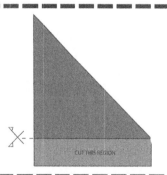

Step 3:

ext, unfold the paper to reveal a square sheet. Fold it in half and then unfold it again to create a center crease. Fold edges A and B towards the center crease, making sure not to cross the center line. Refer to step 3 and step 4 for help.

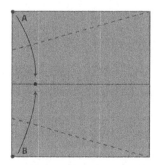

Step 4:

Press down firmly along the creases you've made to ensure your slick slider plane is nice and sturdy. The better you make your creases, the better your planes will be.

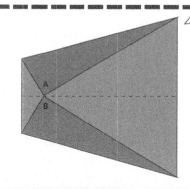

Slick Slider

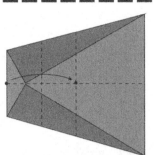

Step 5:
Fold the nose of the airplane from one point to the other, following the arrows as shown.

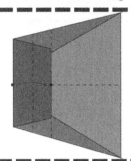

Step 6:
Now, fold along the dotted lines as indicated by the arrows. Remember to make sharp creases each time.

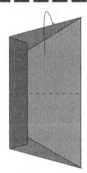

Step 7:
Fold the paper airplane in half along the center line, following the direction of the arrows.

Step 8:
Time to add some wings! Fold the paper down along the dotted lines to create the wing shape. Repeat this fold on the other side.

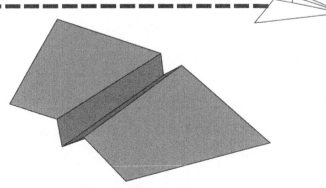

Step 9:
After folding the wings, gently lift them up to create a 'T' shape.
Lastly, bend the tips of the wings slightly upwards for better lift and stability. Now your Slick Slider is ready to take flight!

Let's Make The *Soar Seeker*

Difficulty

★★★★★ **4.0**

Imagine yourself aiming for a world record in creating the ultimate paper airplane. Is it possible? Absolutely!

Creating a top-notch paper airplane isn't too hard, but turning it into a world-class performer takes dedication, science, and serious effort. Brilliant professors have earned doctorates studying paper airplanes. What we know is just the beginning, but there's still so much more to discover! So why not kickstart your journey today with the Seeker?

Step 1:

Place your sheet of paper on the table in a vertical position, like a portrait. Fold it in half from right to left, then unfold it.

Step 2:

Fold the top right and left corners towards the center crease, making sure they don't go over the center line.

Step 3:

Next, bring the right and left diagonal edges to the center crease as shown.

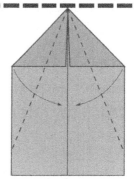

Step 4:

Now, gently pull out the inside hidden sections without unfolding Step 3. Be careful while doing this (Check the picture).

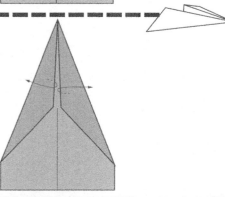

Soar Seeker

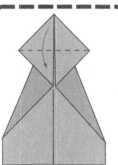

Step 5:
After pulling out the inside corners, your plane should look like the picture. Now, fold down the planes nose along the dotted line shown in here, using it as the center.

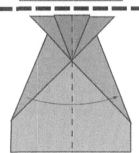

Step 6:
Fold the paper airplane in half along the inside crease as shown.

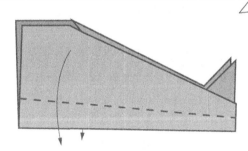

Step 7:
Fold down the diagonal sections to form the wings. Repeat this on both sides (Compare step 7 and step 8).

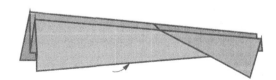

Step 8:
Lift the wings on both sides to complete your Seeker Paper Airplane. Compare step 8 and step 9 for reference.

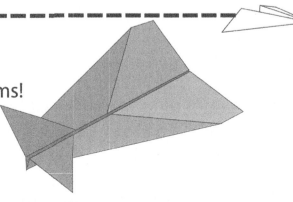

Step 9:
Your Paper Airplane is now ready for action! Give it a toss into the air and see how it performs!

Let's Make The Soaring Spirit

Difficulty

★ ★ ★ ★ ★ 2.5

This guide is all about creating the ultimate paper airplane design, and it all starts with some gentle folds and precise techniques. If you're reading this, chances are you're a paper plane enthusiast just like me! Did you know that statistically, the best paper planes are made from good quality paper?

Make sure to share your thoughts about this awesome book by leaving a review. And don't forget to include a picture of your favorite paper airplane!

Step 1:
Start with your paper lying flat on the table. Fold it in half from left to right, then unfold it.

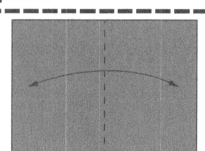

Step 2:
Now, bring the top corners down to the center crease and fold them.

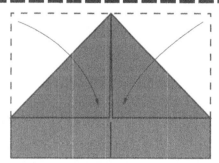

Step 3:
Bring the top point of the paper down to the bottom along the center line and fold it.

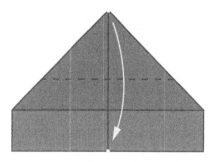

Step 4:
Pull up the folded nose about a quarter of the way up.

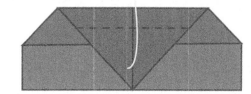

Soaring Spirit

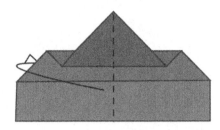

Step 5:
Fold the paper in half along the center crease.

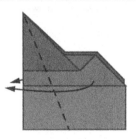

Step 6:
Fold the wings down on both sides, using the dotted lines as your guide.

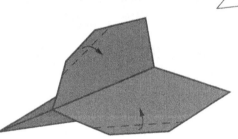

Step 7:
Fold the wingtips upward to create winglets on both sides.

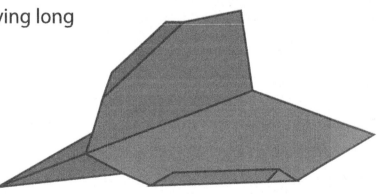

Step 8:
Your awesome paper airplane for flying long distances is now ready to take off!

Let's Make The SOARING SWAN

Difficulty

★ ★ ★ ★ ★ 3.0

Paper Airplane wings may not have the curved shape of real airplanes, but they still fly thanks to their wing angle, known as the Angle of Attack. The Angle of Attack is what creates lift, allowing the airplane to fly. The size of the wings determines how much lift is generated: larger wings mean more lift but slower flight, while smaller wings mean less lift but faster flight.

Now, let's learn how to fold a paper airplane to make the Soaring Swan plane and explore the angle of attack trick!

Step 1:

First, place your paper in Portrait orientation on the table. Fold it in half from bottom to top to make a center crease. Then, fold the top corners down to the center crease to make a mountain fold, like shown.

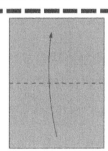

Step 2:

Now, fold the top right and left corners down to the center crease, just like this. Make sure both sides are folded evenly.

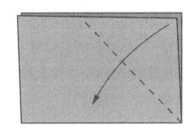

Step 3:

Your paper should look like this. Open it up to look like step 4. Check the comparison between the two figures to make sure you're doing it right.

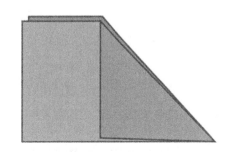

Step 4:

Fold the top part of the paper down to create the nose of your plane. Make sure it's about 3/4ths of the way down the triangle. Align it with the center line of the paper, comparing it with step 4 to step 5.

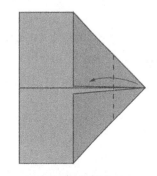

SOARING SWAN

Step 5:
Now, fold the diagonal edges inwards about 1cm on both sides, following the dotted lines as shown. This will help shape the wings of your plane.

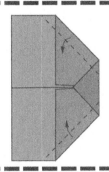

Step 6:
Fold your paper airplane in half along the center crease, creating a mountain fold, just like this. Check to make sure both sides are symmetrical.

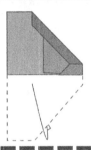

Step 7:
Fold the wings down from the bottom edge about 2cm, as shown in here. Repeat this step for both sides of the plane.

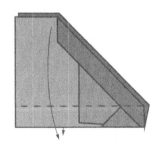

Step 8:
Fold the tips of the wings about 1cm to create winglets on both sides. This will help stabilize your plane during flight.

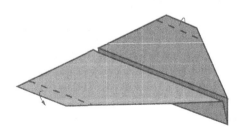

Step 9:
Congratulations! You've made a Soaring Swan paper airplane. Take it outside or find a large indoor space to test its flying abilities!

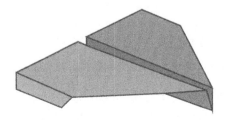

Let's Make The Straight Shot

Difficulty

⭐ ★ ★ ★ ★ 1.5

So, imagine airplane wings are like super special shapes. When the airplane moves through the air, the air above the wings goes really fast, while the air underneath goes slower. This makes the air pressure above the wings lower and the pressure below higher. And guess what? That's what helps the airplane lift off and fly high in the sky!

Now, let's talk about the Straight Shot paper airplane. It's like the superhero of paper airplanes in this book!

Step 1:

Get your sheet of paper and place it flat on your table, like a big rectangle. Fold the left edge over to the right by about 2 cm, creating a valley fold. It should look like the picture.

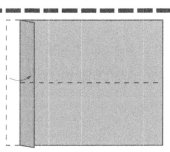

Step 2:

Now, fold your paper in half from bottom to top, making a crease in the center. Then, unfold it.

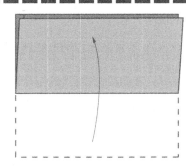

Step 3:

Fold the top left corner and the bottom left corner diagonally towards the center crease you made earlier. And remember, don't cross that center line!

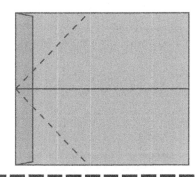

Step 4:

Next, fold the triangle you made in the previous step down along the dotted line, right to the center. Make sure the nose lines up perfectly with the center line.

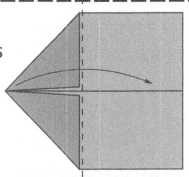

Straight Shot

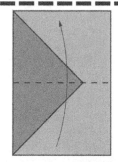

Step 5:
Fold your paper airplane in half again, this time from bottom to top. Check to make sure everything's lined up nicely.

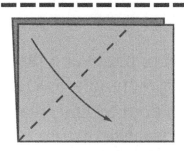

Step 6:
Now, fold down the corners to meet the bottom fold on both sides. Press down firmly to make sure it stays put.

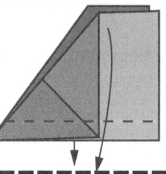

Step 7:
Time to make the wings! Fold them up about 2 cm from the bottom on both sides of the plane. Look at steps 7 and 8 if you need some help.

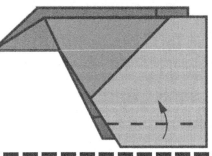

Step 8:
Lift up those wings so they look like a big 'T' shape.

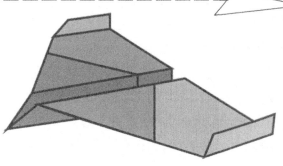

Step 9:
Now, your paper airplane is ready for takeoff! Get ready to launch it into the sky and let it soar!

Let's Make The SUPER DART

Rudders or fins in a paper airplane are like its helpers, making sure it flies straight and true. And guess what? The fuselage, which is the part you hold onto, plays a big role too! It helps keep the plane steady as it flies. But here's the thing: if the rudder is too small or bent, it can mess up the whole flight, causing the plane to spin and crash!

Now, are you ready to make a super dart paper airplane? Let's get folding and see how far we can make it fly!

Difficulty
★ ★ ★ ★ ★ 2.0

Step 1:
First, take your sheet of paper and hold it in portrait orientation. Fold it in half from left to right, making sure the edges meet perfectly. Then, unfold it.

Step 2:
Now, bring the top left-hand edge and the top right-hand edge down to meet the center crease. Make sure they don't cross the center line.

Step 3:
Fold the top of the paper, called the nose, down to meet a straight line drawn across the paper. Match the height from the bottom of the straight line to the bottom of the triangle shape. Once they match, fold the paper.

Step 4:
Bring the top right-hand edge and the top left-hand edge back down to the center crease line. Fold them to make a triangle shape. Look at the picture for step 4 and 5 to help you!

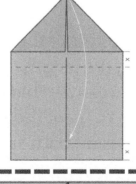
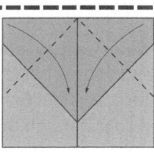

SUPER DART

Step 5:
Fold the top of the nose down halfway to the bottom of the triangle shape. Also, fold the bottom triangle up to lock it in place. Make sure to compare step 5 and step 6 to get it right.

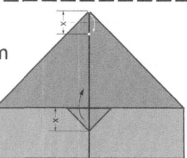

Step 6:
Next, make a mountain fold. Look at the picture to see how it's done.

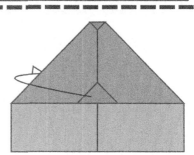

Step 7:
Fold your Super Dart paper airplane in half along the center crease. Check to make sure both sides look the same.

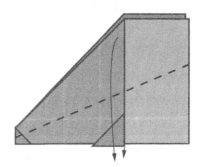

Step 8:
Now it's time to make the wings! The length of the wing should match the length of the fuselage (that's the body of the airplane). Fold the diagonal top section down to meet the straight bottom section. Do this on both sides.

Step 9:
Lift up the wings so they look like a "Y" from the front view and your Super Dart paper airplane is now ready for a sky ride! Give it a gentle throw and watch it soar through the air.
Have fun flying!

Let's Make The Swan Song

Difficulty

★ ★ ★ ★ ★ 2.5

Ever tried making a paper airplane? Yeah, me too! And guess what? Most of mine used to crash right to the ground, nose-first! Pretty funny, right? Maybe you've had similar experiences too! But you know what? Paper airplanes are actually like little engineering wonders! They have to deal with lots of cool stuff like aerodynamics (that's how they move through the air), gravity (that's what pulls them down), and the balance between lift and weight. Sounds interesting, huh?

Step 1:

Lay your paper flat on the table, just like a big rectangle. Now, fold it in half from right to left, and then unfold it. This will give you a nice, straight line down the middle. Next, bring the right and left corners of the paper to that middle line.

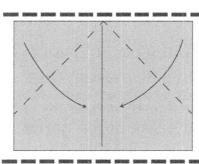

Step 2:

Now, let's do a valley fold! That's when you fold the paper from one dot to another, but towards you this time. Once you've done that, unfold it again.

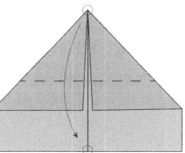

Step 3:

Time for another fold! Yup, fold from dot to dot again, just like before.

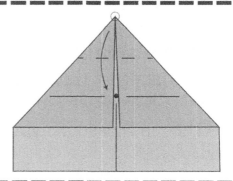

Step 4:

And guess what? We're doing it again! Fold from dot to dot one more time, just like in the picture.

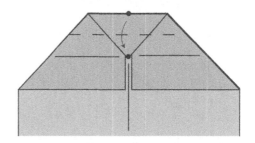

Swan Song

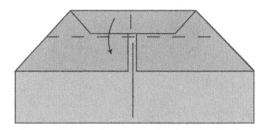

Step 5:
Now, fold the top section of your paper down to that middle crease. If you're not sure, take a peek at the picture to help you out.

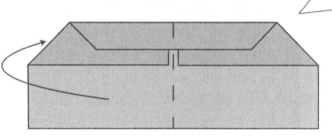

Step 6:
It's mountain fold time! Fold your paper airplane in half, making sure both sides match up perfectly. Symmetry is the name of the game!

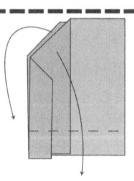

Step 7:
Let's make those wings! Fold along the dotted line, keeping it nice and parallel to the bottom edge of your paper. Look at the picture for some guidance.

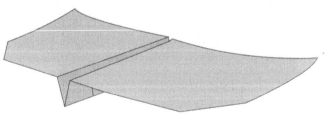

Step 8:
Ready to take flight? You bet! Grab your paper airplane and let it soar through the air. See how far it can go, maybe even all the way across your yard! Have fun, aviator!

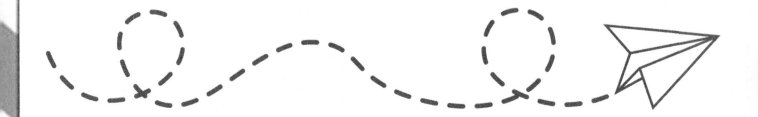

Let's Make
The TRIP
RIPPER

Difficulty

★★★★★ 4.5

Now, we're going to try making a special kind of paper airplane called a glider. It's called a "fatty plane" because it's nice and chunky, like a chubby little bird! Let's give it a try and see how it flies. Are you ready? Let's get folding and soaring through the air!

Step 1:
Place your sheet on the table in portrait mode. Fold the lower right corner 'A' over to the left edge, making sure it lines up perfectly. Then, fold corner 'B' over to meet the other corner 'A'. Make sure to crease the folds well and then unfold.

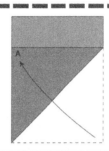

Step 2:
Now, fold corners A and B to meet the crease upside down.

Step 3:
Make sure to crease the fold from step 2 really well for a better flight. Then, unfold it.

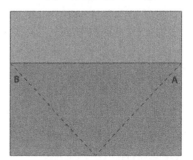

Step 4:
Gently push the paper inward along the arrows on both sides towards the top. The lower section will automatically meet the center.

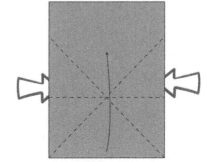

TRIP RIPPER

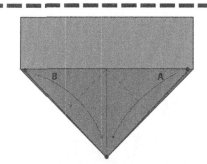

Step 5:
Fold corners A and B to the dot on the lower edge of the center line. If you're still confused, take a look at step 6.

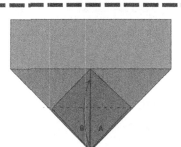

Step 6:
Now, fold the plane's nose back to the bottom. Make sure to crease it firmly and straight.

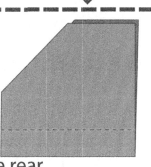

Step 7:
Fold the plane inside to get a structure like the picture. Now, let's make the wings! Fold along the dotted lines on both sides all the way down. Then, unfold to make a shape like a 'T'. You'll see the 'T' shape when you look at the paper airplane from the rear.

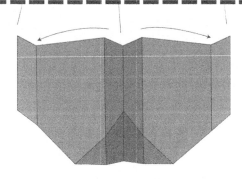

Step 8:
One of the coolest parts of paper airplanes is the winglets! Fold about 1cm vertically on both sides of the wings. And there you have it - your awesome Trip Ripper paper airplane is ready for action!

Let's Make The VALKRYIE

Did you know that different paper airplane designs need different ways to launch them? It's true! Just like how each airplane looks different, they also have their own special launching styles.

For example, delta wing planes like to be thrown really fast and hard. They need lots of speed to fly their best! But glider designs are a bit different.

So, let's learn about the Valkyrie by throwing it into the air! But wait... we have to make one first, don't we?

Difficulty

★ ★ ★ ★ ★ 2.0

Cutting to a Square:

Keep your sheet vertically like a portrait rectangle over the work table or floor. Grab the top right sharp edge to match the left side of the paper straight. Now cut off the bottom remaining piece of the paper with scissors.

Cut This Off

Step 1:

Fold your paper in half from right to left, and then unfold it. Next, bring the top right-hand edge and the top left-hand edge to the center line to make a cone shape, just like in the picture.

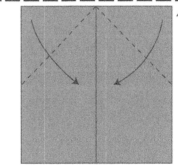

Step 2:

Now, fold the nose of your Valkyrie down to where the previous fold ends. Make sure the top point of the nose matches the center line perfectly, and then unfold it.

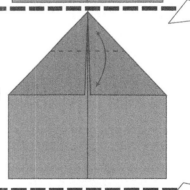

Step 3:

Fold the nose to the backside using the crease you made earlier. Remember to keep those edges nice and straight!

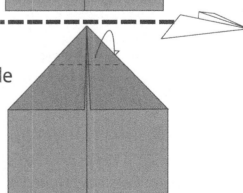

VALKRYIE

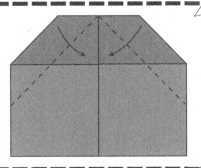

Step 4:
On both wings, fold the sides in to create a peaked tip, Look at step 5 for refrence.

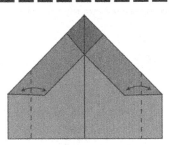

Step 5:
Next, make a mountain fold. Look at the picture to see how it's done. Then on both wings, fold the winglets inward and then unfold them.

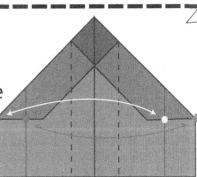

Step 6:
To make the primary wing, fold the outside corners of the left and right sides. Then, unfold them. Flip the paper over and get ready for the next step.

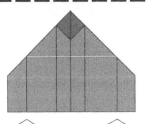

Step 7:
You've already made the crease lines needed for the dihedral wing shape. Now, fold them as shown for the perfect wing shape.

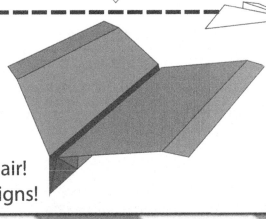

Step 8:
The Valkyrie is ready for action! Test it out at different speeds and angles to see how far it can fly.
What are you waiting for? It's time to take your Valkyrie to the ground and let it soar through the air! Enjoy making and flying more paper airplane designs!

Let's Make The *Wind Ripper*

Difficulty

★★★★★ 2.5

When I was in school, my uncle made a super cool paper airplane that flew really far! It went about 5-7 meters! I was so amazed and asked him how he did it. Later, I learned that to make planes fly far, they need to be just right. They have to be the perfect shape and have something called aerodynamics, which is like the magic that makes things fly smoothly through the air. But guess what? We're not just going to talk about it. We're going to make it!

Step 1:
First, put your paper on the table with the long edges at the top and bottom. Fold it in half from right to left and then unfold it. Next, fold the top left corner over to the right edge and make sure it's folded neatly.

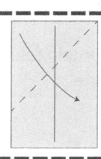

Step 2:
Now, look at the picture and fold point A to the left side along the dotted center line. Press down to make a good crease.

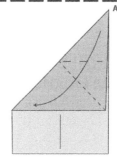

Step 3:
Now, fold point A down to meet the center line. Match the dots together and press down firmly to make a strong crease.

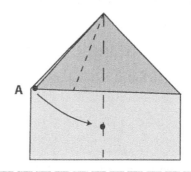

Step 4:
Tuck point A inside the upper triangle shape and make sure it stays in place.

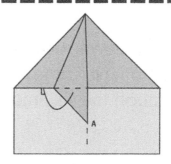

Wind Ripper

Step 5:
Fold the top dot down to the bottom dot, following the direction shown. This fold is called a valley fold.

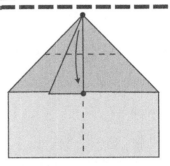

Step 6:
Next, make a mountain fold. Look at the picture to see how it's done.

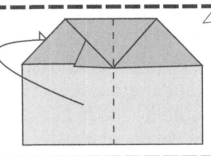

Step 7:
Fold the plane from dot to dot, making sure it's folded evenly. Do the same thing on the other side.

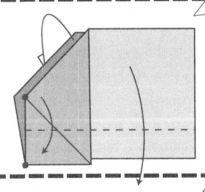

Step 8:
Now, you'll see a triangle shape at the bottom. Fold it up to make a winglet.

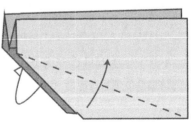

Step 9:
You did it! You made a cool fly fold paper airplane! Now, it's time to have some fun! Take it outside and let it soar through the air. Enjoy the magic of flying!

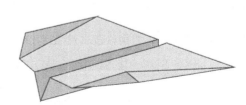

Let's Make The *Wind Whisper*

Difficulty

⭐⭐⭐⭐⭐ **4.0**

What makes birds really special compared to other animals? It's their amazing ability to fly! Sure, some insects and even snakes can fly too, but let's be real – nothing can beat the grace and speed of a bird in flight. And just like birds, airplanes and aircraft can also take to the skies. But you know what's really cool? Paper airplanes! They're like tiny, low-cost aircraft that you can make yourself. Today, we're going to learn how to make a paper airplane called the Wind Whisper. It's super easy to make, loads of fun to play with!

Cut the Square:

First, grab your sheet of paper and hold it up vertically like a tall rectangle. Make sure it's nice and straight on your table or floor. Now, take the top right corner and fold it over to match the left side of the paper. Next, grab some scissors and carefully cut off the bottom part of the paper.

Cut This Off

Step 1:

But before we start, let's make sure our paper is a square. Fold it diagonally from right to left, then from top to bottom, and unfold it. Now, bring the top corner to the center point, and do the same with the bottom corner.

Step 2:

Now, fold the two folded edges to their opposite edges.

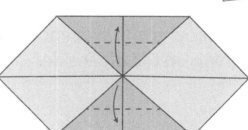

Step 3:

Now, flip the paper over to the other side. You'll see the result of your folding!

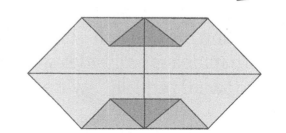

Wind Whisper

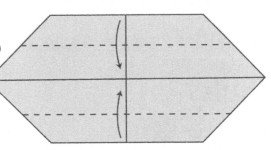

Step 4:
Bring the top and bottom folded corners to the center horizontal crease and fold them.

Step 5:
Fold the plane in half as shown,

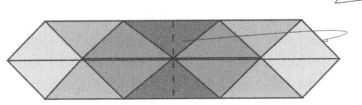

Step 6:
Make the wings by folding them down with an approximate fuselage length of 1.5 to 2 centimeters.

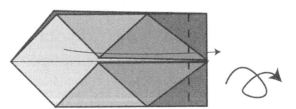

Step 7:
Flip the paper plane over and do the same thing on the other side.

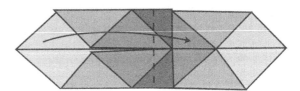

Step 8:
Lift both sides of the plane equally upwards and make sure it's dihedral in shape. That means both sides should be angled upwards equally. Awesome job, pilots!

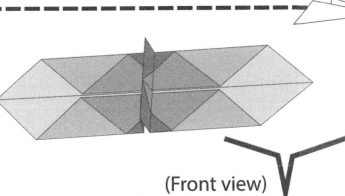

(Front view)

Let's Make The Winter Wind

There are lots of different paper airplane designs out there, but what makes them fly? Let me give you an example. Me and my friend Bruce Wayne were trying to make a plane by just folding a piece of paper and crushing it, then throwing it as far as we could. But Bruce didn't think it was a real paper plane! Why not? Well, paper planes need to cut through the air smoothly and create something called "lift" to stay up in the air. But when you crush the paper, it creates a lot of "drag," which slows it down.

Difficulty

★ ☆ ★ ★ ★ 1.5

Step 1:

First, fold the paper in half from top to bottom to create a center crease. Then, bring the bottom left corner up to the center crease, following the white line, crease it well!

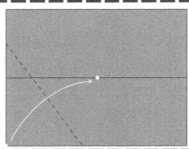

Step 2:

Similar to Step 1, bring the top left corner down to the center crease, following the white line and dotted line as shown in the picture.

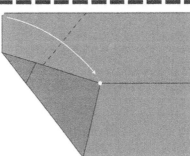

Step 3:

Now, in any orientation you like, fold the top and bottom corners to meet at the center point marked by white dots. Make sure to create firm creases with each fold.

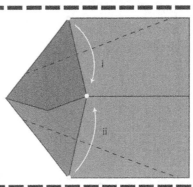

Step 4:

Bring the nose (marked with a white dot) back to the starting point like shown here.

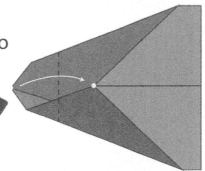

Winter Wind

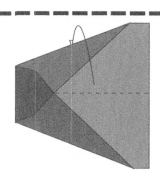

Step 5:
Fold the paper airplane in half along the center crease, as shown here.

Step 6:
Take the folded edge of the plane and fold it upwards to create the wings. Make sure the wings are larger than the fuselage (the middle part of the plane). Repeat this step on the other side to ensure they match.

Step 7:
Unfold the wings slightly upwards, resembling the front view of the airplane. Now, your Winter Wind plane is ready for some fun flying! It's sure to perform well at the evening party!

(Front View)

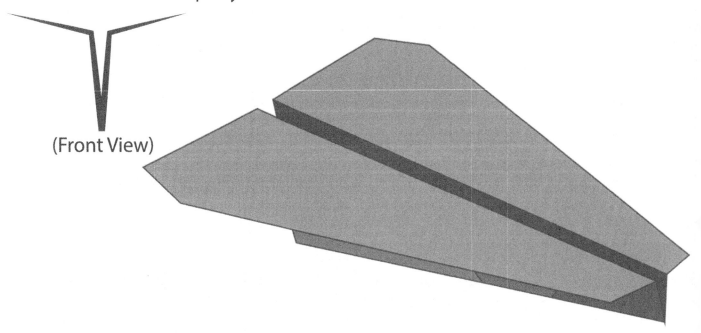

As a small family, we want to express our heartfelt gratitude for choosing to purchase our book. Your support means the world to us, and we genuinely appreciate it. If you enjoyed reading our book, we kindly ask you to leave a review on Amazon and share a photo of your favorite paper airplane that you created. Your feedback and participation mean everything to us. Thank you once again for your support and happy flying!

From our family to yours,
    THANK YOU!

Made in the USA
Las Vegas, NV
24 October 2024